Dor

May 2013 be
a blessing!

K

Doris

Many hours of pleasure
in blessings.

Be Still? Really, Lord??

Surviving Unexpected Losses and a Long Desert Season with my Smile and Laughter Intact!

By
Kris Cavanaugh
ICF Certified Coach
Speaker & Trainer
Shift Inc.™

www.BeStill-ReallyLord.com
www.BeginToShift.com

Copyright © 2013
Kris Cavanaugh
All Rights Reserved

No part of this book may be reproduced or transmitted in any form or by any means, electronic or mechanical, including photocopying, recording, or by any information storage and retrieval system, without permission in writing from the publisher. Permission to quote brief excerpts for review is granted without further permission when accompanied by publication data.

Disclaimer: This book contains advice and information. The publisher and author disclaim liability for any psychological or medical outcomes that may occur as a result of any of the suggestions in this book.

Published by Shift Inc. (www.BeginToShift.com)
Atlanta, GA
ISBN 978-0-9849855-1-7 (paperback)

Cover design, illustrations and book graphics created by Danny Cavanaugh, owner of Cavanaugh Designs. Danny's website is www.CavanaughDesigns.com.

For more information email Kris@BeginToShift.com or call 404-551-3601.

DEDICATION

This book is dedicated to all the people who actively participated in my journey through my 2012 desert by praying for me or providing a variety of support along the way…especially my parents, who have been a rock of encouragement each step of my journey.

Table of Contents

INTRODUCTION: 7

DESERT BEGINNINGS 8

LITTLE DEATHS 12

SEEKING A NEW FAITH COMMUNITY 15

TRUSTING IN G_D, DESPITE MY CHECKBOOK BALANCE! 21

DIVINE INSIGHT FROM LEFT FIELD 26

EXPERIENCING G_D 29

I HEAR YOU! 33

HOW I KEPT MY SMILE & LAUGHTER INTACT 113

THE END OF MY STORY ? 117

FINAL THOUGHTS 118

COACHING & TRAINNG 119

ABOUT KRIS CAVANAUGH & SHIFT 122

LEGAL DISCLAIMER 124

RESOURCES CITED 125

INTRODUCTION:

I'm always amazed that my life can feel entirely normal for a significant period of time, and then WHAM....all of a sudden "normal" disappears and in its place appears a life I don't quite understand. I know you can relate....and maybe even be experiencing that very feeling right now.

This book was born about eight months into my desert season, and at this time I have no idea how the ending will turn out. My hope is, by the time I get ready to publish this book, I will have a happy ending to share. Except our Lord does not promise happy endings – instead, all He promises is that He'll be with us every step of the way.

I would encourage you to read this book from front to back instead of skipping chapters, that way you experience my journey the same way I did - allowing G_d to speak to you in stages…just the way He spoke to me.

When you are done reading this book, please send an email to *Kris@BeginToShift.com* to let me know how G_d spoke to you through the re-telling of my desert journey.

May our Lord allow this book to be an encouragement to you - regardless of how difficult or far-gone your circumstances may feel – in order to help you find <u>your</u> smile and laughter throughout your pain, and let you experience the "peace that passes all understanding" (Philippians 4:7)[1].

~ Kris Cavanaugh

PS - For those of you wondering why I spelled G_d with an underline instead of an "o"…that spelling comes from my season in a Messianic Jewish/Gentile Congregation: It shows a deep sign of respect for our Lord's name[2] (see Resources Cited section at end of book for more information).

DESERT BEGINNINGS

Whether you see it coming or you unexpectedly crash into it, a desert season is a period when your life, as you once knew it, no longer exists and left in its place are typically confusion, loneliness, emptiness, extreme discomfort, and directionless wandering. Most people experience a desert season at least once in their lives.

G_d uses our desert experience to deepen our faith, mold new character traits, develop new truths deep within us, or even as a preparation period for future divine assignments. The time we spend in the desert varies, but as we learned from Moses and the Israelites, our human frailty might cause it to be far longer than G_d intended. My desert season began in 2012.

Similar to the previous four years, 2012 started off for me with the normal client and business building activities, in addition to investigating other sources of income. What I didn't know then is that within a month my life would turn completely upside down.

Back in December 2011, I took some time to mentally create a list of goals I wanted to accomplish in 2012 (if you've known me for any length of time, you'll know it is in my DNA to set goals, create strategic plans, and then give everything I have and more to accomplish them). So when January 2012 arrived, I began to coordinate my life to make those goals a reality.

One of those goals pertained to my relationship with my husband, Danny. If you've read any of my previous books or articles, you already know our nine years of marriage had many ups and downs. We had always managed to pull through our difficulties and strengthen our marriage along the way. However, there was one area with which we still struggled…and I was bound and determined that 2012 would be the year we would FINALLY get it right.

Due to various things going on during the beginning of the year, January flew by and it wasn't until the weekend before Valentine's Day that I saw an opportune time to chat with Danny. I knew the conversation would be difficult, but I also knew that we had survived those conversations before – why should now be any different?

About an hour into the conversation my intuition bells started going off, but I couldn't put my finger on exactly why things didn't feel right. We ended the conversation some time later with an agreement that we both wanted to continue to work through our issue, and set up a time to get together again with suggestions for how to proceed.

When we sat down again, it took about thirty minutes before I knew the moment I had been dreading for nine years was about to become a reality as soon as I heard Danny say, "I'm more afraid of leaving this marriage than I am of staying in it."

It became crystal clear at that very moment that somewhere in the last two years Danny had decided our marriage was broken and nothing we could do would fix it. Knowing Danny as well as I did, I knew he had not yet recognized the finality of those words, which is why I responded, "Being more afraid of leaving is no reason to stay in our marriage. I know we can get through this, but I can't do it alone. So you are going to have to make a decision as to whether you are in, or whether you are out. It's going to take serious work on both our parts, and it's not fair to either of us for you to stay if you do not really believe we can overcome our issue."

After he avoided my eyes for a while I asked him how he wanted to proceed, and more than a minute went by without an answer. I responded by saying "We've been married too long for you not to know the truth about how you feel deep down in your heart." The silence continued until he asked for more time to think. I knew the time he needed was not to be sure about his answer, but rather to generate the courage to actually say the words. So I sighed and told him to let me know his decision in the morning.

The rest of the day we pretty much avoided each other as much as we could in our small house. I went to bed early and he went to bed very late. We faced different walls, and I could literally feel the distance grow exponentially between us. Neither one of us got any sleep, though no words were said, so I got up at 6 AM to let the dogs out, and sat at the kitchen table for a very long time.

Around 9 AM that Sunday morning Danny came downstairs and avoided my eyes again as he began to make his breakfast. I just sat and watched him. Several minutes went by with him still avoiding my eyes and not saying a word. Finally, I said with tears in my eyes, "What is your decision? It's not fair to keep me waiting because I know you've already made it."

When Danny turned to look at me, he had tears in his eyes and I heard the words he had said many, many times before…*but this time I knew he meant it*: "I'm done. I just can't do this anymore. We've tried several times and I just don't believe it will ever get fixed."

The last two times we had this conversation (2006 and 2008) I refused to give up on him or us, and managed to convince him to continue to try to make it work. This time, however, was different. The moment he said those words I felt G_d's peace within me finally giving me permission to let him go, despite the agony of my heart ripping in two. I knew Danny had nothing left in him to save the marriage, and it was time to release him without a fight.

As the tears began rolling down my cheek, I told him that he would need to initiate the divorce in order to get the process started and that I would not contest it. Then I walked away to begin actively grieving a marriage we had worked so hard at saving for nine years.

After moving into the spare bedroom that afternoon and having yet another sleepless night, Monday began with a difficult rollercoaster of complex emotions starting with a conversation with my friend to ask him to step in as my divorce lawyer once Danny initiated the process, followed by a phone call to my parents to give them the sad news. They loved Danny like a son and they were heart-broken for both of us.

The rest of February and March consisted of multiple (and mostly amicable) conversations between Danny and I and our lawyers around the division of assets and liabilities until the settlement was finalized and sent to the judge in late March. In Georgia, the minimum amount of time a divorce can be processed is 30 days (if there are children or asset/liability disputes, it typically takes much longer). Ironically, had the judge not sat on the paperwork for two weeks, the divorce would have been finalized at the 30 day mark by the end of March – but as it turned out, April 17th was the day our divorce legally became final.

I moved out on April 9th (I didn't want the house and felt strongly I needed to start over in a new place). Then, sometime in late May it became very clear that G_d was not only releasing me from my marriage, but He was also removing every bit of my old life as well. Thus began an additional series of losses and a lengthy grieving period as I continued my unexpected trip into the desert.

LITTLE DEATHS

Merriam-Webster defines grief as, "a deep and poignant distress caused by or as if by bereavement."[3] I believe that definition comes up short. If I were to define grief it would be: *"an emotional rollercoaster in which you feel as though you are drowning and treading water at the same time, along with experiencing multiple little deaths at every turn."*

Shortly after I moved into the spare bedroom while Danny and I were negotiating our divorce settlement, I began to come face to face with the realization that I was grieving more than just the loss of my marriage. Every time I turned around I realized I had lost something else in the process, which felt like yet another death I was forced to deal with. Every time those moments arrived, I acknowledged them as a "little death" and continued to swim through those grief moments as well.

For example, once I decided to let Danny have the house and started looking for a new place to live, it became painstakingly clear that I was going to have to pay far more than I wanted to in order to live in an area where I felt comfortable. I can't tell you the number of times I met a real estate agent at a rental apartment or house, or did a drive by and just stared, despondent and weeping, at how little I would be getting for the money I would need to spend in a part of town I did not like.

After 20 plus rental showings, I finally found an apartment with a garage to secure my motorcycle within a neighborhood I could comfortably rebuild my life. I was in a bit of shock when I found out I'd be paying $300 more than my mortgage for 1/3 the space, but at that point, I was exhausted at searching and decided I'd rather buy fewer groceries and go without some other things than spend one more ounce of energy continuing my search for a new place to live. So I signed on the dotted line and trusted G_d would provide the finances to cover my rent.

Other little deaths I experienced included the lack of a constant companion; having to shop for one instead of two; realizing there was no one to help me set up electronic stuff or deal with mechanical issues; having to check the "divorced" box on a variety of forms as I set up my new life; and not feeling at home, but knowing I was home, day after day in the apartment.

Two additional significant little deaths I had to grieve through were 1) leaving my dogs behind (I refused to keep two 60-lb Huskies in an apartment – they needed a yard - and asked Danny to care for them until I was able to afford another house), and 2) receiving clear direction from G_d to "lay down my business" and serve someone else.

So in the course of three months I lost my marriage, my dogs, my house, and my business, leaving me in a state of complete financial insecurity. I had no idea how I was going to make ends meet, but knew I wasn't alone. G_d had always paid my bills in the past, and I had an amazing support network to lean on as I emotionally journeyed through my uncertain future.

The inner strength I always knew I had and used in the past came out in full during this time. Instead of helplessly wallowing in my pain, I accepted it and allowed myself to get lost in it at times to work through my grief, but also used my strength to step out of my pain as needed to effectively function on a day to day basis.

Also, because I was able to manage my grief well, I could actually see the humor in my situation and often laughed (sometimes very sarcastically) at new levels of perception and understanding I NEVER would have gained had I not gone through this experience.

For example, before the divorce I always chuckled good-naturedly at people who included visitation rights to their pets, because how does one say good-bye to a furry-child? Then, when it happened to me, not only did I chuckle - I laughed out loud with complete understanding because I was now stepping in their shoes. To this day I laugh inside when people I know smile that "I kind of get it, but not really" smile I used to give to others whenever they see me getting excited about going to visit my girls (my two Huskies) for a few hours. That lesson alone helps me remember never to assume I completely understand anything until I've walked a mile in someone else's shoes.

Many times during April I sarcastically said to my friends and family that the best thing about my situation was instead of losing everything at different times and feeling pain over and over, I was actually thankful G_d ripped away everything at the same time so I would only have to deal with the pain once. *Better the pain of one HUGE band-aide being ripped off, than multiple small ones* – at least in my opinion!

.

SEEKING A NEW FAITH COMMUNITY

When I moved, I left my church behind as well and began to search for a new faith community. I was invited by a friend to check out Andy Stanley's Buckhead Church campus and really enjoyed it, but something told me that G_d wanted me to keep searching. A few days later, a thought popped into my head and I was reminded of four previous times throughout my adult life where I felt a pull to connect with the Jewish roots of my Christian faith. In the past, each time that pull appeared I did not take the time to investigate it. However, this time I had nothing but time to kill - so I did.

I did a search through Google for "Messianic Jewish Synagogue in Atlanta," wondering if anything would show up (after all, I figured there couldn't be that many Jewish people in Atlanta who believed Jesus was the Messiah). To my surprise, several Messianic congregations were within 30 minutes of my apartment, and several more were located across Georgia[4]. The closest congregation to my apartment was in Tucker, GA: Beth Adonai Congregation[5]. I contacted Judy, the Rabbi's wife, and invited her out for a cup of coffee. She graciously accepted and a few days later I spent almost two hours asking her question after question about Messianic Jewish beliefs and the community as a whole.

The entire time I was with Judy it was as though G_d was speaking through her to me. I felt like I had uncovered a treasure chest of knowledge I had been seeking my whole life, but never knew existed. I still had no idea why G_d wanted me to move in that direction, but I also knew that I was not going to let the opportunity pass me by yet another time.

I attended my first Messianic service the following Saturday and the moment I walked in the door I knew G_d was calling me to use my desert season to immerse myself in Him through Jewish lenses. I began a weekend practice of going to Synagogue services on Saturday morning and then either attending Buckhead Church live or virtually on Sunday!

Continuing to immerse myself, I began buying and inhaling books and articles to educate myself about the Jewish foundation of my Christian faith, and investigated Messianic Jewish claims that Old Testament celebrations and Torah guidelines were not cancelled after Jesus' resurrection. I subscribed to online newsletters from a variety of Messianic organizations. I watched online videos from previous Beth Adonai Shabbat services and morning teachings.

It was as though I became the man from the Gospel of John who spent a lifetime being blind and then in an unexpected moment was given the ability to see (John 9:25: "One thing I do know is that I was blind, but now I see"). G_d had opened wide a new door of knowledge into my life for a reason, and I was going to inhale as much of it as possible while the door remained open.

In addition to a crash course in my Messianic Jewish education, G_d also led me to inhale messages from Andy Stanley's church community. Several years of sermon videos are hosted on their church website, and I spent marathon hours watching topics that interested me. Each hour I spent with G_d through Messianic and Christian messages was time spent deepening and widening my knowledge, altering my perspective, and growing me to a new level of faith in Him. My desire to learn and grow was insatiable...my spirit wanted more and I had been blessed with time to satisfy those wants.

By July, I consistently had one foot in the Messianic world and one foot in the Christian world, building a community of new friends in both. I often wondered why G_d wanted me in both, but decided until He told me to choose I would straddle both sides – though I did make the decision to become a member at Beth Adonai and give my monthly tithes to support them.

If you asked me what I love most about the Messianic Jewish/Gentile community, I would tell you it is their passionate celebration and connection to G_d's Word. The Jewish people as a whole (Messianic or not) grow up in a culture where the Torah (G_d's Word) is an integral part of their life. However, just as in Christian communities where there are many "Easter & Christmas" Christians, so too in the Jewish Community there are many "High Holy Day" Jews. The difference, in my opinion, is that the importance of the Torah is ingrained into the Jewish people from birth, regardless of whether they are practicing Jews or not….whereas Christians do not actually have a connection to G_d's Word until they become a regular part of a Christian community.

Let me explain that another way. The culture around anyone's up-bringing defines the foundations of who they are at their core. As they grow older, they make choices about that foundation to either deepen it or alter it as needed, based on the wisdom they gain through life experiences. In a nutshell, the foundation itself becomes the springboard for a person's life – our choices then become our direction.

If our foundation sets up a default based on G_d's Word, we then can't help but move in that direction until our choices divert us elsewhere. Practicing Jews honor G_d's command to *"Fix these words of mine in your hearts and minds; tie them as symbols on your hands and bind them on your foreheads. Teach them to your children, talking about them when you sit at home and when you walk along the road, when you lie down and when you get up. Write them on the doorframes of your houses and on your gates, so that your days and the days of your children may be many in the land the* LORD *swore to give your ancestors, as many as the days that the heavens are above the earth"* (Deuteronomy 11:18-21).

The Torah is a constant companion to practicing Jews and celebrated in the Jewish culture from birth. Non-Jews (or Gentiles, as we are called) do not typically grow up with that kind of ingrained pull towards G_d's Word (the Torah). Instead, we Gentiles often come to

G_d's word through choice, not through a cultural and metaphorical "DNA" default pull.

This became very clear during my experience of attending High Holy Day celebrations at Beth Adonai. One of the celebrations is called Simchat Torah (or "Rejoicing of the Torah") and is the culmination of Sukkot. It celebrates the ending of the annual Torah reading cycle[6] and the beginning of a new cycle [In Jewish culture, Torah has different meanings including: 1) scripture as a whole, 2) rabbinical teachings, 3) traditional Oral Law and, in its narrowest definition, 4) the first five books of the Bible. In this case, "Torah" cycle refers to the first five books of the Bible].

During the Simchat Torah celebration, the Torah scrolls are carried around the sanctuary seven times and the congregation typically dance and sing songs as they follow the Torah around the sanctuary. Later in the service, several members of the congregation read a part of the Torah, ending with the last parashah (a section of scripture) of Deuteronomy followed by the first parashah of Genesis.

As I was watching the reverence and celebration of G_d's Word, the first thought that came to mind was, "Why don't we celebrate G_d's Word like that in the Christian community?" In my Christian experience, most churches revere scripture and encourage everyone to dive into its wisdom…but "celebrate" the Bible? Never once can I remember a whole Christian service or holiday season focused on "celebrating" scripture…all of our celebrations and holidays were focused on Jesus or G_d….not the Word itself. I walked away from that service knowing I had just uncovered a deep truth which I did not yet understand completely.

A few months earlier, I had attended the HaYesod[7] class to continue my education of G_d's word from a Jewish perspective. HaYesod is a Hebrew word that means "the foundation." HaYesod teachings are non-denominational. First Fruits of Zion created the program in 1998 to address a growing interest in the Jewish origins of the Christian faith.

In the workbook I received, the stated purpose of HaYesod is as follows: "The HaYesod discipleship program attempts to educate believers on their relationship with the Promised Land, the historic people of God, and the Scriptures of the Jewish people. Knowing the Jewish foundation of Christianity deepens the faith of the believer, clarifies the meaning of the Bible, and reveals God's purpose for all His people....It is our goal to bring clarity, understanding and unity through these teachings to the body of Messiah as she recognizes her place and role within the greater community of Israel" (page xiii)[8].

I thoroughly enjoyed the HaYesod program and was surprised several times when I realized my perception of a scripture verse or a Christian concept wasn't quite accurate when held up again the original Hebrew translation of those very same words. It seemed that some of my long-standing perceptions had to change based on new truths G_d had revealed through the HaYesod program, while others were strengthened.

I feel honored to be a Gentile worshipping alongside Jews knowing that through Yeshua (the Hebrew name for Jesus) I am *"grafted in among the others* [Jewish People] *and now share in the nourishing sap from the olive root*" (Romans 11:17), and *"This mystery is that through the gospel the Gentiles are heirs together with Israel, members together of one body, and sharers together in the promise of Christ Jesus"* (Ephesians 3:6).

Even though Scripture makes it clear that the Jewish people are G_d's chosen people, it does not mean we Gentiles are "less than." Like any adopted child, our Father (G_d) does not love or treat us any differently. However, the promises of G_d were entrusted to the Jewish people first and must be honored no matter how many children come after. I'm just glad that G_d in his mercy is allowing us Gentiles to receive those promises through our relationship with Yeshua.

I have been in the Messianic community for over eight months now and am so glad G_d gave me the privilege of being a part of this amazing learning experience. As I said earlier, it has deepened and widened my faith on many levels – so much so that I purchased a piece of jewelry called a Messianic Seal to represent my growth. The Messianic Seal is a symbol used by James the Just (the brother of Jesus) and the 12 Apostles in Biblical times which represented joint congregations of Jews and Gentiles worshipping together as Jesus-Believers. The ancient three-part symbol includes the Menorah, the Star of David, and the Fish. If you are interested in learning more about the Messianic Seal, go to Amazon.com and type in product #9652229628. The charm I bought is product #B003T85F6Y.

TRUSTING IN G_D, DESPITE MY CHECKBOOK BALANCE!

I want to back up several months in my story to give you the full-picture of my 2012 desert experience. What you don't know is that despite having a successful business helping people achieve their personal or professional goals or transform their lives, my business was not profitable. Like any new business I expected it to take a few years to turn a profit – but then the economy tanked in 2009 and my services were then perceived as a luxury item by most people [despite all the research that coaching and other professional/personal development programs actually help people make money and achieve more success in the long-run…but alas, I digress! ☺].

Now, I must give credit where credit is due. Danny was incredibly supportive when I told him I wanted to start my own coaching business in 2007. He knew when I committed to anything, I was ALL IN and would do whatever it took (within moral boundaries anyway) to achieve success. He agreed to cover all the bills until the business turned a profit. Year after year I got closer and closer, but year after year I couldn't quite get to a point of being able to pay myself.

In February 2012, when Danny and I began the divorce process, I took a good hard look at my personal and business expenses - within seconds I knew I was in trouble. I had no income and no way to pay those bills. Not only that, but the red tape around the financial part of the divorce settlement took much longer than I expected and the money was not released to me until almost 10 weeks later – leaving me with very little money in my checking account as I moved out of the house.

In late March, shortly before my scheduled moving date, I called my business CFO for advice (which just happens to be my Dad). He raised me to be an independent woman and taught me how to budget and be financially responsible. As I was dialing his number, I knew how he would respond - but it was important for me to hear his voice to help me begin the process of what I knew I had to do.

I started out the conversation the way every business owner would when talking to a CFO in this type of situation: "So (short pause), I reviewed the books and there's not much money left – how do you suggest I proceed?"

Dad, in his typical CFO manner, responded back as only Dad would, "Well, honey – it's not my company. I just take care of your books. How do you want to proceed?" - which is exactly what I knew he would say because he also taught me to take responsibility for my future, no matter how bleak it may look the moment.

I sighed and began to recount how I had been in business for almost five years and each year was financially better than the last...but for some unknown reason G_d had not blessed me with financial prosperity. I also acknowledged that I did everything right: I hired the right consultants, implemented the right marketing and sales initiatives, and had the privilege of being a transformation catalyst to 1000s of people through my coaching programs, speaking engagements, and products...and yet STILL I could not break profitability.

Dad patiently listened to me as only a father would and when I paused long enough for him to talk he said, "So what do you want to do?" I sighed again and wished this could be one of those times I could crawl into his lap and let him take charge of my future...but alas, I am an adult businesswoman and with that comes grown-up responsibilities.

"Maybe G_d has other plans for me? Maybe this business was a stepping-stone to some other career path? Maybe I should shut it down and find a (gulp) full-time job working for someone else?" I said sadly...and then suddenly said hopefully, "But then again, maybe

G_d will bless the business once I move out and begin rebuilding my life?"

"That's entirely possible," responded Dad, "So how do you want to proceed?" Once again, Dad was gently reminding me he was not going to make a decision for me. I was the business owner and it was up to me to steer the ship. His job was to make sure I didn't crash into anything.

I told Dad I felt it was time to put out a "fleece" because I had no idea how to proceed and needed a concrete answer about G_d's intentions for my future since everything in my life was currently out of my control (go to the www.BibleGateway.com website and type in Judges 6 on the search bar to read about Gideon's story of doubting G_d's promise and how he asked G_d for a sign to relieve his doubt using a fleece in the desert). Dad supported my idea and I set my fleece date as May 31st. Until then I would run my business as usual and honor all my commitments to my clients and network.

My "fleece" prayer was simple: "Lord, you know I've done everything in my power to make my business profitable. You also know that the divorce is going to leave me with no financial support to pay my bills. Within that knowledge I also know everything I have is yours and you have never once come up short in helping me pay my bills. However, I see no logical way to make ends meet and certainly do not have any opportunities coming up to fill in the financial gaps. So I am asking you to honor my fleece request: on May 31st if you want me to continue forward with my business efforts, please provide a long-term contract that will cover my personal and professional expenses. If you have other plans for me, then do not provide the money and give me insight about what my next career path may be."

March ended and April began with my bouncing between intense grief around the divorce and stepping out of that grief long enough to honor my commitments as a coach to my clients and as a business woman to my network. At first, very few people knew what I was going through because I was skilled at leaving my grief at home once I stepped into role of coach or business owner. Those that did know remarked at how well I was handling everything – to which I responded that "I" wasn't doing anything…G_d had gifted me with an abundance of supernatural inner peace which was allowing me to function effectively for the most part.

From March through May I would ask G_d every day to honor my heart's desire to keep the business open, but also acknowledge that HE was G_d and knew better than I did how my future should unfold. Despite His silence, I felt my spiritual intuition preparing me for the answer I did not want to hear.

As the weeks went by, my checkbook balance dropped to almost zero and I had to call Danny twice to ask his permission to advance me money that he agreed to pay through the settlement at a later date. I hated making those calls. I had to swallow my pride several times, and take great care not to yell at G_d in anger for allowing me to be in a situation in which I had no financial stability.

As May 31st approached, I was hopeful that my G_d of miracles would come through for me, and yet also at peace that if He didn't, everything would be okay – despite my sadness around that possibility.

On May 31st I stayed near the phone and checked the mail for some sort of "Hail Mary" answer to prayer. No checks came in the mail and no phone calls were received to finalize a business deal. By 5 PM I closed my computer, resigned that G_d had clearly answered my fleece prayer and it was time to grieve yet one more loss in my life.

I began to proactively look for a job on June 1st and felt G_d calling me to use my skills and talents to make someone else successful. I knew if I was going to work for someone else, that person had to have characteristics and morals I respected – in addition to having a management style I felt comfortable working under. After thinking long and hard about how to describe this type of person in order to tap into my network to find him or her, it dawned on me that he or she would best be described as a Servant Leader.

The term "Servant Leadership" is contributed to Robert Greenleaf based on his book, *The Servant as Leader*[9]. After researching the term, I describe this type of leadership style as: a leader who leads by serving others first to make sure those people achieve their goals, thus laying a foundation for success and goal achievement at all levels of the organization…which ultimately makes it easier to lead in the long run.

Once I determined I wanted to work under a Servant Leader, I began to contact my network to set up meetings to pick their brains about people they knew who fit that description. I had a goal of scheduling 100 meetings over three months and was very busy (and on track) to make that happen…until just after meeting number 60 when G_d diverted me with an unexpected answer to prayer.

DIVINE INSIGHT FROM LEFT FIELD

Walking in faith can sometimes feel like driving your car on a desolate country road surrounded by a thick fog. You can't see where you are going and must slow down enough to focus on the white lines on the road in order to keep your car from running off a cliff. The thicker the fog, the slower you have to go.

I don't do "slow" very well. My personality type is results driven and the quicker they are achieved, the better. When I am pushed into circumstances that do not allow me to move at my desired pace, I default to working really hard at creating an opportunity for movement, and then run at full speed in that direction.

From February through August my entire life was foggy. I had no idea what my future held and every day I was living in faith that G_d would pay the bills. My regular prayer during that timeframe was this: "Lord, I trust you have me in the palm of your head, but it would be great if you could provide clarity and direction about how to move forward with my life because I'm really tired of living in the fog of uncertainty."

As I said earlier, it's in my DNA to establish goals, create strategic plans, and then work hard to achieve them. One of my goals after the divorce was a commitment not to even consider dating anyone until January 2013 to give myself about a year to grieve through the loss of my marriage and heal any subsequent wounds so that I would not bring that baggage into my next relationship. Part of my plan to ensure I was emotionally ready to date was to schedule an appointment with the therapist Danny and I had used on several occasions throughout our marriage.

The purpose of that appointment was pure and simple: I needed an objective perspective from someone that had journeyed through our marital difficulties and seen me at my emotional worst; who also knew my trigger points and would have no problems shooting straight with me about how to move forward from being a wife for nine years to being a divorced woman ready to date.

During the appointment our conversation ran the gamut of topics (mostly because I hadn't seen him in almost three years and we had a lot to catch up on), but the most significant was when I started telling him about how I was dealing with G_d's silence with regard to my career search. I shared that my usual method when making important decisions is to reach out to my support network for their advice, then spend time in prayer, followed by a period of waiting for G_d to give me clarity around my decision. Then, after a period of time (each time is different) if I don't get an answer from G_d, I decide which direction I think is best for me and ask G_d to close doors if I am heading down the wrong path. I knew it always seemed to work for me in the past, and so I was confident it would work again now.

After sharing that information, my therapist smiled at me and asked if he could take that concept into a similar scenario to discuss it further. I had no idea why he wanted to do so, but trusted he had a reason – so I agreed.

He began by saying, "Let's pretend that you have a decision to make and you've reached out to your support network for advice. However, the people you value most have been really busy and unable to give you their feedback. Would you move forward without their input?"

I didn't even hesitate for a second and blurted out, "Of course not. I would drive to their houses, call them at odd hours, or do whatever I could to get their opinion before moving forward because I know what they have to say is important feedback in order to make a good decision."

My therapist once again smiled and then asked me the most profound question I've had in a long time: "Why then would you not give G_d the same respect?"

A light bulb instantly went on in my head and suddenly I realized that sometime in the last 20 years I had created a habit of running ahead of G_d when I experienced His silence. How then could I ask Him to guide me through the fog of my current life circumstances so I could make good decisions around my career, finances, and eventually dating relationships if I wasn't going to wait for His answers? Without even knowing it, I was laying the groundwork through that pattern to potentially complicate my already unstable and uncertain future.

And G_d - in his humorous way - used that moment to finally answered my "give me clarity and direction" prayer (the one I had been praying for weeks) - not by giving me an clue about my future, but rather by helping me see how I was preventing Him from answering my prayer due to my impatient reaction to His silence.

I can only imagine my therapist laughing in his head (good-naturedly, off course) at the look on my face when I finally realized what I was doing. How could he not? I often have that same good-natured laugh run through my head when my clients have light bulb moments during our coaching meetings at the moment they realize something I had seen before they did.

Once I overcame the shock at realizing how off track I had gotten with regards to praying for God's direction and not waiting for His answer, my therapist suggested I read a book that would significantly change my life: *Experiencing God*[10] by Henry & Richard Blackaby and Claude King.

EXPERIENCING G_D

The moment I arrived home from my therapy appointment I ordered the *Experiencing God* book from Amazon. I have a Prime Membership (that $79 membership is one of my greatest discoveries) which meant it would arrive in my mailbox two days later.

Strangely enough, the conversation at the therapist's office was in line with previous conversations I had been having with several other people around the subject of "hearing from G_d." I truly desired a more intimate relationship with G_d and wanted that communication to be TANGIBLE.

I know people who have ongoing and tangible conversations with G_d all the time. We can be talking about anything, and suddenly they'll look upward and either ask a question or state something – and G_d will answer them *right then and there*. These are people I have come to trust, so I know they are not making it up.

Over the last few years I've wanted that kind of relationship with my Lord. I want our communication and relationship to FEEL as though He was physically standing in the room and I could see Him.

A few weeks before my therapy appointment, I was talking with a woman who has that type of relationship with G_d, and lamenting that no matter how hard I tried, I couldn't seem to "hear" Him the way she did. I was especially frustrated because my desert season required His voice to see my way out.

When the *Experiencing God* book arrived in the mail I inhaled it within 48 hours. My greatest moment of insight was when the authors made it abundantly clear that none of the other prophets or men of faith ran around asking G_d why they didn't get a burning bush. They accepted that G_d would speak to them uniquely and never even conceived at comparing G_d's communication style with others to how He communicated with them.

At my core, I recognized I was essentially demanding of G_d, "Where's my burning bush?" because I was envious (in a good way) at how He was communicating with other people I knew. The lessons in the *Experiencing God* book completely changed my perception and laid the groundwork for Him to answer my "clarity and direction" prayer – but, as usual, not in the way I expected.

About half way through the book, the authors suggest starting a journal to keep track of scripture verses and other ways G_d reveals His direction, and new or revised truths about Himself or His ways. This journal is an important element of ensuring that we are hearing G_d correctly, and becomes a written testimony of that communication when difficult life circumstances cause doubt to creep in.

The authors make it clear that in addition to scripture, G_d will often confirm His communication through prayer, circumstances and the church body. He is always working around us – most of the time we just can't see it. It is always a blessing when He chooses to reveal what He is doing around us so that we can join Him in that work.

I started my journal on September 1st not knowing what to expect. Part of me doubted that G_d would speak that quickly – after all I had been praying for my "burning bush" communication for a very long time without any response.

Before I actually tell you what transpired, I need to preface this story a bit. For years I have subscribed to a number of devotions via email or bought devotional books. I always read them in the morning and often enjoyed them and gained a new perspective, but rarely ever felt the voice of G_d communicating directly to me. Because of that, my devotion time had become a routine and I treated it as such. I didn't jump out of bed excited about reading G_d's Word or someone's commentary on a Biblical topic. I did it because I knew it was something I should do.

The morning of September 1st I sat down with a hardbound journal I had been meaning to give to someone who would appreciate it (I do not like to journal), and wondered when G_d would start speaking to me tangibly.

God's humor arrived in full force within seconds. My first devotion of the morning was an email distribution from *Wisdom Hunters*[11]: The scripture for that day was "*My sheep listen to my voice; I know them, and they follow me.*" (John 10:27). I laughed out loud at His acknowledgement that He was indeed speaking to me at that very moment (and probably had been all along, but I had not been paying attention).

My second devotional from *The Upper Room*[12] continued that theme: "*My child, be attentive to my words; incline your ear to my sayings. Do not let them escape from your sight; keep them within your heart...*" (Proverbs 4:20-27, NRSV) and "*Stand at the crossroads and look; ask for the ancient paths, ask where the good way is, and walk in it, and you will find rest for your souls...*" (Jeremiah 6:16). I laughed again at the reminder to "be attentive to my words" and ask for "the ancient paths."

The last communication I received that morning from G_d was from my Messianic Torah study: "*Wait for the Lord; be strong and take heart and wait for the Lord*" (Psalm 27:14).

I looked upward upon reading those words and said in absolute awe, "I HEAR YOU! I promise to try very hard not to run ahead of you anymore and instead wait for your direction"

G_d showed me that morning He had chosen to communicate with me primarily through scripture (and I wanted a burning bush! Can you see me trying to pack one of those in my purse and taking it with me everywhere?). Later I would begin to notice confirmation or encouragement of that communication through circumstances and other people.

In addition to writing down what you hear G_d communicating to you in your journal, the *Experiencing God* authors also suggest you end your journal entry each day with a personal prayer based on what G_d shared with you. My prayer that September 1st morning was as follows:

Lord - Thank you for the "light bulb" moment so I can change my pattern of decision making to wait for an answer from you instead of assuming you'll close doors as I move forward. Thank you for having my therapist suggest the "Experiencing God" book so I can recognize your voice more clearly - and (hopefully) more often - to develop the intimate relationship I desire to have with you. Continue to strengthen my "G_d ears, eyes, and intuition" so that I can hear you, see you, and sense you working in my circumstances – as well as other's circumstances – to support you in your work however I can.

Almost daily from September 1st onward G_d spoke to me through scripture and various other resources. The next part of this book is focused on what He said and what I learned, along with the prayers I lifted up to Him.

I HEAR YOU!

The following is a copy of my journal so you can see how I managed to keep my laughter and smile intact during my desert season while G_d spoke to me through sermon series, Torah Club[13] studies, a variety of devotions (*Wisdom Hunters, Streams in the Desert*[14]*, The Upper Room,* Sharon Jaynes' e-zine[15]*, Learning to Live Above*[16]), the *Experiencing God* companion workbook[17], *God's Promises to His Children*[18]*, Appointment in Jerusalem*[19]*, Prayers that Avail Much*[20], and other materials (see "Resources Cited" section).

Because I was reading G_d's Word from so many sources, I began to notice several themes through similar scripture verses over the course of a day. I did not go looking for any of the verses listed in my journal…*He delivered them all to me*.

My circumstances at the start of writing this journal are as follows:

- I have no personal income and am living off just what I received in the divorce settlement
- I am still unsure of what career path I should take
- I am still emotionally grieving the loss of my marriage, dogs, house, business, and a variety of other losses I experienced as G_d allowed my old life to be completely ripped away…leaving me in a season of complete uncertainty.

As you read the journal, you'll notice I chose to be completely open about the sadness, frustration, anger, and joy I experienced. My G_d is big enough to handle the full range of my human emotions, and only through being honest with Him was I able to process those feelings, hand them over, and heal.

My hope is that my willingness to be vulnerable with you will allow you, in turn, to be vulnerable with others the next time you journey through your own desert season or challenging situation.

My Journal Entries

NOTE: Italicizes within scripture are my emphasis and anytime you see, "..." it means I skipped over a part of the scripture passage in order to focus on the core message of what G_d was saying to me.

9/2/Sun

<u>What G_d Said:</u>

"There is a time for everything, and a season for every activity under the heavens:...a time to kill and *a time to heal*; a time to tear down and *a time to build*; *a time to weep and a time to laugh*; *a time to mourn* and a time to dance...*a time to search* and a time to give up...a time to tear and *a time to mend*; *a time to be silent and a time to speak*...What do workers gain from their toil? I have seen the burden God has laid on the human race. He has made everything beautiful in its time." (Ecclesiastes 3:1-11A)

<u>What I Learned or Was Reminded About:</u>

- This grief-filled uncertain time is a season – not forever.
- G_d has a reason for remaining silent with regards to my future and will speak it into existence in His time.
- No matter how far gone a circumstance may feel, G_d makes everything "beautiful" eventually.

<u>What I Prayed:</u>

Lord – As I continue to wait in this transitional period of my life to see what career doors you open, I thank you for the reminder that there is a season for everything and that you will make my life "beautiful" again at some point. Thank you for the peace you've granted me as I wait for your perfect timing, and trust in this extended period of time you've given me to heal from my divorce and prepare me for your next life assignment.

9/5/Wed

<u>What G_d Said:</u>

"Yet you know me, O Lord; *you see me* and test my thoughts about you." (Jeremiah 12:3A)

"Praise to the Lord, to God our Savior, *who daily bears our burdens*." (Psalm 68:19)

"For this reason, since the day we heard about you, we have not stopped praying for you and asking God to *fill you with the knowledge of his will through all spiritual wisdom and understanding.* And we pray this in order that *you may life a life worthy of the Lord and may please Him in every way*: bearing fruit in every good work, growing in the knowledge of God, being strengthened with all power according to his glorious might so that *you may have great endurance and patience,* and joyfully giving thanks to the Father, who has qualified you to share in the inheritance of the saints in the kingdom of light." (Colossians 1:9-13)

<u>What I Learned or Was Reminded About:</u>

- You see me and know what is going on, even when I don't feel like you do.
- Your desire is to bear our burdens for us - if we would remember to give them to you.
- Knowledge of your will comes through time in your Word.
- The more time I spend with you, the easier it is to live a life worthy and pleasing to you in my everyday world.
- Great endurance and patience is always available through you.

<u>What I Prayed:</u>

Lord – Thank you for dying for my sins so that I can come into your presence whenever I desire. Thank you for bearing my burdens so I can focus on my daily life with full assurance that you are working behind the scenes to lay a foundation for my future. Please show me your will through spiritual wisdom and understanding so I can clearly see how to move forward with my life in order to live a life worthy of your sacrifice and be pleasing to you in every way. I surrender my will to you because you know me, see me and have tested my thoughts about you – allowing me to fully trust my future to you.

9/9/Sun (early morning)

What G_d Said:

"The Lord will send a blessing on your barns and on everything you put your hand to. *The Lord your God will bless you in the land he is giving you.*" (Deuteronomy 28:8)

What I Learned or Was Reminded About:

- My blessings are coming – don't doubt it!

What I Prayed:

Lord – I am expectantly waiting for the "land" you are preparing for me. I thank you for this time of preparation as I wait. I love you and know you have me in the palm of your hand and will provide answers and blessings in your time.

****

9/9/Sun (late day)

What G_d Said:

A secure faith is built on the *promises* of God…God is capable of helping us, but is not obligated to anything other than the promises He made in scripture [like receiving "mercy" and "grace" from Hebrews 4:16]…God often uses our pain and circumstances to grow our faith as an example to others, and to bring them to faith. So we should have faith in God, not our circumstances, and thank him for being *for me* and not against me – regardless of how you feel in your circumstances. (paraphrased from *Saving Faith*[21] sermon series, Part 2)

"And the glory of the Lord will be revealed, and all mankind together will see it…" (Isaiah 40:5A)

Sometimes our selfishness [what we want] is camouflaged in how we expect God to reveal His glory. (paraphrased from *Saving Faith* sermon series, Part 3)

What I Learned or Was Reminded About:

- Trust in what G_d has already promised to me, not what I want Him to do.

- Keep watch for the glory of God in my circumstances.
- Don't deceive yourself or God – make sure your desires/intentions are full of integrity.

<u>What I Prayed:</u>

Lord – I'm guilty of camouflaging my selfishness by expecting you to reveal your glory through giving me the high-income job, house and dogs before the end of the year. I am NOT happy where I am, so I want you to make things better in my whole life. I know you know best, and yet still, "I WANT!"

Please help me to REALLY surrender my wants and praise you for the opportunity to show your glory through my faith walk amidst my frustration. Let me depend on and receive your mercy and grace in my time of need. Help me to be content where I am until another door opens, regardless of how long it takes (SCARY THOUGHT…what if it doesn't happen for a long time???).

You know what I want. Help me to want, and to be at peace, with what YOU want for me.

9/10/Mon

<u>What G_d Said:</u>

"However, as it is written: No eye has seen, no ear has heard, *no mind has conceived what God has prepared for those who love him*." (1 Corinthians 2:9)

"Two things I ask of you, O Lord; do not refuse me before I die: Keep falsehood and lies far from me; give me neither poverty nor riches, but *give me only my daily bread*. Otherwise, I may have too much and disown you and say, "Who is the Lord?' or I may become poor and steal, and so dishonor the name of my God." (Proverbs 30:7-9)

<u>What I Learned or Was Reminded About:</u>

- There will always be things I don't understand because I am not capable of thinking like G_d.
- All I need is enough daily bread to meet my basic needs - anything above that is a want and not necessary.

<u>What I Prayed:</u>

Lord – As I live in my holding pattern, my human mind has planned outcomes a plenty! However, I know your plans are greater than mine ever could be. I am unable to conceive what you are preparing for your daughter that loves you. I would much rather trust in your future than mine – even though my impatience wants it to happen now. Help me to continue to "be still and know you are G_d" for as long as it takes.

Let me be content with whatever YOU determine is my daily bread instead of my desire for a high paying position to cover what I WANT to have in my life. My wants are surrendered to your will and plan for my life. Please reveal those plans to me as quickly as possible.

Be Still? Really, Lord??

9/11/Tue

What G_d Said:

"*I will repay you for the years the locusts have eaten…*You will have plenty to eat, until you are full, and you will praise the name of the Lord your God, who has worked wonders for you…" (Joel 2:25 A and 26A)

What I Learned or Was Reminded About:

- G_d will restore what I lost during my desert season in His own way (which may not be my way).
- Sometimes you have to swallow your pride and take a position in which you are completely overqualified (example: Restaurant Server) for a season, trusting you'll end up where you are supposed to be at some point in the future.

What I Prayed:

Lord – I soooo desire that you restore all that has been lost this year (an income to live on / a house to live in / my dogs who I miss terribly). I trust however you choose to "repay me" will cause me to be content and overjoyed with your generosity. Keep me focused on how I can serve others while I am waiting on you. Thank you for the money you provided from the divorce settlement to pay the bills and the money I will generate while working at Taco Mac as a Server over the weeks to come.

9/12/Wed

What G_d Said:

"And so *after waiting patiently*, Abraham received what was promised." (Hebrews 6:15)

What I Learned or Was Reminded About:

- I'm being called to wait on G_d and I will receive His promises in His time.

What I Prayed:

Lord – Thank you for the reminder that I will receive your promises in YOUR timing. Help me to continue to manage my impatience until that time arrives. Thank you also for the members of the Oasis[22] group [Divorce Recovery program through Buckhead Church] who have become friends over the last 13 weeks.

9/14/Fri

<u>What G_d Said:</u>

"Now to him who is able to *do immeasurably more than all we ask or imagine*, according to his power that is at work within us…" (Ephesians 3:20)

<u>What I Learned or Was Reminded About:</u>

- Don't limit G_d.

<u>What I Prayed:</u>

Lord – Thank you for the reminder that your blessings and management of my life is always going to be far better than I could ever imagine. I remain at peace in my holding pattern (desert season) until you choose to open the door to my next career path.

9/16/Sun

<u>What G_d Said:</u>

"…hide in the Kerith Ravine…" (1 Kings 17:3)

> "Every saintly soul that desires to wield great influence over others must first win the power of some hidden "Kerith Revine. Acquiring spiritual power is impossible unless we hide from others and ourselves in some deep ravine where we may absorb the power of the eternal God." (*Streams in the Desert,* 9/16 commentary).

<u>What I Learned or Was Reminded About:</u>

- Deserts and ravines we sometimes end up in give us an opportunity to grow and learn.

<u>What I Prayed:</u>

Lord – I desire to have a career in which I "wield great influence" and I know in that type of career I must be deeply grounded in your Word and better able to sense your leading. Thank you for my time in my 2012 "Kerith Revine" in which I have lost everything and been forced to lean on you for everything. Help me to quickly learn and grow however I need to so that I may step out of my Ravine into my new life, and bring glory to you in the process.

9/19/Wed and 9/20/Thu

<u>What G_d Said:</u>

"…my Father is the gardener. He cuts off every branch in me that bears no fruit, while *every branch that does bear fruit he prunes so that it will be even more fruitful.*" (John 15:1-2)

"Then Jesus said, 'Did I not tell you that if you believed, you would see the glory of God.'" (John 11:40)

> "…*you do not have to understand all God's ways of dealing with you*. He does not expect you to understand them. You do not expect your children to understand everything – do you? You simply want them to trust you. And someday you too will see the glory of God in the things you do not understand." (*Streams in the Desert*, 9/20 commentary).

<u>What I Learned or Was Reminded About:</u>

- I should feel blessed when I am pruned by you.
- Stop trying to understand G_d. Just trust that He IS G_d.

<u>What I Prayed:</u>

Lord – I'm wired to seek understanding and can bear anything if I know why I'm experiencing it. I've been struggling lately with the "why's" of my life. I don't know what you are doing behind the scenes, but I am tired of where I am and just want to move forward with my life.

I totally trust you have my best interests with your overall strategy, but your methods frustrate me! Please provide whatever internal resources I need to hang on while you continue to prune me to your satisfaction…and help me be content along the way.

9/21/Fri

<u>What G_d Said:</u>

"…Lord, *I want to see*…" (Luke 18:41)

"For *in him* we live and move and have our being." (Acts 17:28A)

<u>What I Learned or Was Reminded About:</u>

- My greatest desire is to see where G_d is leading me.
- Only "in Him" will I find the best life can offer.

<u>What I Prayed:</u>

Lord – I thank you for showing me your presence through a variety of scripture and devotional readings over the last few weeks. I do desire to "see" you, but I think I want more to feel and hear you. Please expand my "G_d senses" so I may deepen my intimacy with you.

9/22/Sat

What G_d Said:

"Who despises the day of small things?" (Zechariah 4:10A)

> "Small things are big to God, so they are not to be discounted or despised…therefore do not despise this season of small things. They are like seeds that eventually grow into grand and glorious opportunities of influence…Your savior is stringing together a sequence of small activities that lead to larger outcomes. So stay with the small things, for in due season you will reap the harvest." (*Wisdom Hunters* / "Small Things")

What I Learned or Was Reminded About:

- Be content doing the small things for G_d's glory.

What I Prayed:

Lord – Let me become just as excited to journey through the "small things" you want me to experience as I am with the big things. I trust I can live out my purpose in the mundane as well as the exciting times. Keep my G_d eyes and ears attentive to your direction every day.

9/23/Sun

What G_d Said:

"Keep your lives free from the love of money and *be content* with what you have, because God has said, 'Never will I leave you; never will I forsake you.'" (Hebrews 13:5)

What I Learned or Was Reminded About:

- "Be content" seems to be a running theme I need to pay attention to.

What I Prayed:

Lord – I am sensing that you REALLY want me to learn how to be content in whatever circumstances I am placed. I know you will never leave me or forsake me, and will also provide the means to journey through my circumstance – no matter how long it takes…even if it is a lifetime.

I'm a doer, Lord. You gave me "Type A" DNA…so sitting and waiting is not my strong suit. It never has been. I get the feeling that THIS season of waiting is significant, and that I will miss what you have for me next if I rush through it.

Thank you for teaching how to manage my impatience all of these years to prepare me for THIS moment in time…THIS season of uncertainty…so that I am better prepared to learn the lesson I need to learn around "Being Still" and waiting on you.

Continue to remind me to wait through your Word, other people, and circumstances…because my "Type A" personality will continue to want to run ahead of you.

I love you, Lord. Thank you for whatever you have prepared for me next.

9/24/Mon

<u>What G_d Said:</u>

"When they came to the border of Mysia, they tried to enter Bithynia, but *the Spirit of Jesus would not allow them to.*" (Acts 16:7)

"…He wakens me morning by morning, wakens my ear to listen like one being taught." (Isaiah 50:4B)

<u>What I Learned or Was Reminded About:</u>

- You are calling me to be still and wait for as long as it takes.

<u>What I Prayed:</u>

Lord – I'm becoming more and more certain that my mantra during this season is "Be content where I am and wait on you to open the next door of my life." Whenever I doubt or whenever my "Type A" personality becomes frustrated, remind me that your timing is best…that ultimately this earthly experience is temporary in the big scheme of eternity with you. Certainly I can handle any temporary circumstance. I trust you, despite what my human tendencies desire. I will continue to manage my human wants while I am following my spiritual intuition.

9/25/Tue

<u>What G_d Said:</u>

"'For I know the plans I have for you,' declares the Lord, 'plans *to prosper you* and not to harm you, plans to *give you a hope* and a future.'" (Jeremiah 29:11)

> "God has made a place for you to fit perfectly within His plan, but sometime we have to wait in an uncomfortable place until he opens the door. *Do not go searching desperately for your place* because God will show you where it is if you trust and wait on Him." (*Learning to Live Above* / "Finding Your Fit" p. 19)

<u>What I Learned or Was Reminded About:</u>

- Why am I scurrying around frantically trying to find a job when G_d has made it clear that He wants me to "BE STILL" and wait on Him?

<u>What I Prayed:</u>

ALRIGHT….I hear you loud and clear. Thank you for the reminder and confirmation that I am NOT to proactively look for a job at this time. I am to passively wait and be still until opportunities to network or apply for jobs come to me.

Being passive is not in my DNA either, so I am assuming you are strengthening that spiritual muscle for a reason. I trust that my desert experience will bear fruit later and I will continue to find joy and be content where I am.

The best thing about all the time I have on my hands is that I can use it to learn more about you through my Bible Study group, Torah Club classes and devotions, etc. What a blessing! Thank you for my desire to learn.

Be Still? Really, Lord??

9/26/Wed

<u>What G_d Said:</u>

"Do not lag in zeal, be ardent in spirit, serve the Lord. *Rejoice in hope, be patient in suffering, persevere in prayer.*" (Romans 12:11-12, *New Revised Standard Version translation*).

"Be still and know I am God…" (Psalm 46:10A).

"We live by faith, *not by sight.*" (2 Corinthians 5:7)

"…*Like clay in the hand of the potter*, so are you in my hand, O house of Israel." (Jeremiah 18:6B).

<u>What I Learned or Was Reminded About:</u>

- Suffer patiently; still my emotions; don't live by sight or through my feelings.

<u>What I Prayed:</u>

Lord – I'm thankful that you have helped me grow my faith over the years to the point that my emotions (for the most part) can take a back seat to my faith. The only emotion I'm struggling with right now is my "drive to DO SOMETHING!"

Thank you for the reminder that this is my season to do NOTHING, other than what you bring to me. I continue to be still and trust that you will restore all that I've lost in whatever form you choose to restore it…and that it will be the best for me at the right time.

9/27/Thu

What G_d Said:

"*Fix these words of mine in your hearts and minds*; tie them as symbols on your hands and bind them on your foreheads…Write them on the doorframes of your houses and on your gates." (Deuteronomy 11:18 and 20)

"Your word is a lamp to my feet and *a light for my path*." (Psalm 119:105)

"Jesus replied, 'What is impossible with men is *possible with God*." (Luke 18:27)

What I Learned or Was Reminded About:

- Time spent in the Word is critical and valuable to light my path.
- Anything is possible for G_d.

What I Prayed:

Lord – Thank you for your Word and for finally allowing me to "hear" you through it regularly (it only took 44 years!). I trust that all things are possible with you, and I continue forward through my desert with peace in my heart.

9/29/Sat

What G_d Said:

"Forget the former things; do not dwell on the past. See, *I am doing a new thing*! Now, it springs up; do you not perceive it? *I am making a way in the desert* and streams in the wasteland." (Isaiah 43:18-19)

"Some trust in chariots and some in horses, but *we trust in the name of the Lord our God*." (Psalm 20:7)

What I Learned or Was Reminded About:

- Even though I can't see it, you are creating "a new thing" in my life through my desert season.
- Don't trust in anything except G_d.

What I Prayed:

Lord – You are a G_d of renewal, and I completely trust in you. My eyes are on my future, and I await your direction knowing that you are making a new way in the desert for me.

9/30/Sun and 10/1/Mon

<u>What G d Said:</u>

"I have learned the secret of being content in any and every situation, whether well fed or hungry, whether living in plenty or in want. *I can do everything through him who gives me strength.*" (Philippians 4:12B-13)

"...*Give careful thought to your ways*...You expect much but see, it turned out to be little. What you brought home I blew away. Why?...Because of my house which remains a ruin, while each of you is busy with his own house." (Haggai 1:7 and 9)

> "...they [God's people] have become too busy with their own stuff and forgot about Him...In His presence, there is great joy, supernatural peace, and overwhelming love. There is no striving or stress, no frustration or worry – just Him...When we position ourselves in His presence, opportunities will seek after us, instead of us seeking them." (*Learning to Live Above* / "Going Out of Busyness" p. 41)

<u>What I Learned or Was Reminded About:</u>

- Be mindful of my actions, trusting that only God can give me strength.

<u>What I Prayed:</u>

Lord – If there's one thing that has been true for 2012 it is this: I have NOT been busy. This lack of busy-ness has given me tons of time to spend with you via sermon series online, Bible Study, devotions, and new friendships. Thank you for the blessings of my desert experience. I know I am in the right place when I am in your presence.

The quote "opportunities seeking after us" really spoke to me. My nature is to make things happen and I am uncomfortable sitting still and doing nothing. I WANT opportunities to seek after me! Let me continue to trust that will happen as I sit still in my desert season.

Be Still? Really, Lord??

10/2/Tue

What G_d Said:

"…Then he took them with him and they *withdrew by themselves*…" (Luke 9:10B)

> "Come with me by yourself and rest a while…in my quiet strength be strong…the bread of life is here for you to eat and here for you the wine of love to drink…*those brief hours are not lost in which you learn more of your Master and His rest in heaven.*" (*Streams in the Desert*, 10/2 commentary)

"Trust in the Lord with all your heart and *lean not on your own understanding*; in all your ways acknowledge him, and *he will make your paths straight.*" (Proverbs 3:5-6)

What I Learned or Was Reminded About:

- Time with G_d gives me a better understanding of how to make my paths straight.

What I Prayed:

Lord – Thank you for all the hours I am spending with you alone in my desert. I don't understand the reasons behind it, but trust you are making my paths straight and that eventually you will allow me to finally see those paths – because I certainly don't right now.

10/3/Wed

What G_d Said:

Seeking an understanding of what Paul meant by "content" in the Philippians 4:11-13 passage, I spent time researching it. During that research, G_d led me to *Matthew Henry's Commentary* on the Bible. According to the online version, "content" means Paul brought to mind his condition and made the best of it with an even temperament, and was not tempted to distrust God or go his own way when experiencing afflicted conditions[23].

What I Learned or Was Reminded About:

- Content is not a feeling of happiness!

What I Prayed:

Lord – Thank you that I don't have to be happy about my desert season and losses (because you know I'm not)…just that I have to be at peace in my heart, soul, and mind - trusting you are here with me working behind the scenes as you hold me in the palm of your hand.

10/4/Thu

What G_d Said:

"*We wait in hope for the Lord*; he is our help and our shield" (Psalm 33:20)

> "David was anointed and experienced the power of God, but it was over 20 years before he became King….Jesus works out His will while you wait." (*Wisdom Hunters* / "Called to Wait")

"*The Lord blessed the latter part of Job's life more than the first.*" (Job 42:12A)

"In this you greatly rejoice, though now *for a little while you may have had to suffer grief in all kinds of trials*. These have come *so that your faith* – of greater worth than gold, which perishes even though refined by fire – may be proved genuine and *may result in praise, glory, and honor* when Jesus Christ is revealed." (1 Peter 1:6-7)

> Job was looking for answers everywhere…"He could not find God in any direction he searched, but came to the conclusion that God 'knows the way I take' (Job 23:1-10)…Job trusted God and decided that he would stay the course until God came to him." (*Learning to Live Above* / "Testing in Progress" p. 52)

"…I will make your name great…" (Genesis 12:2B)

> "Nothing is more pathetic than having a small character when you have a big assignment…He [God] may want to adjust your life and character in smaller assignments first to prepare you for the larger ones." (*Experiencing God* companion workbook / Unit 2, Day 5)

What I Learned or Was Reminded About:

- There is always a reason for a waiting season - particularly character building to prepare for future assignments.
- G_d blesses those who wait on Him and praise Him despite challenging trials.

What I Prayed:

Lord – Today the theme seems to be "character building." I trust you know who I need to be and what I'm capable of enduring – which is why you are leading me through my 2012 desert.

I am learning on a deeper level to trust in you: Every season of difficulty NEVER goes wasted by you. I know you are with me and will open a door to be released from my desert at the perfect time.

10/5/Fri

<u>What G_d Said:</u>

"About Benjamin he said: 'Let the beloved of the Lord rest secure in him, for he shields him all day long, and *the one the Lord loves rests between his shoulders.*" (Deuteronomy 33:12)

<u>What I Learned or Was Reminded About:</u>

- I am the Lord's child and can rest in Him at any time.

<u>What I Prayed:</u>

Lord – Thank you that I have the privilege of being able to crawl into your lap and place my head between "your shoulders," leaning on your chest like a little girl, when I need to feel secure and at peace. Thank you for my desert time with you and for the additional character traits you are building to prepare me for my next assignment.

10/7/Sun (morning)

<u>What G_d Said:</u>

"…Let him who walks in the dark, *who has no light*, trust in the name of the Lord and rely on his God." (Isaiah 50:10B)

"But they *who wait for the Lord* shall renew their strength; they shall mount up with wings like eagles; they shall run and not be weary; they shall walk and not faint." (Isaiah 40:31, English Standard Version translation)

"Do not be anxious about anything, but in everything, by prayer and petition, with thanksgiving, present your requests to God. And the *peace of God, which transcends all understanding*, will guard your hearts and your minds in Christ Jesus (Philippians 4:6-7)

"Don't be 'owned' by worry. Pray and petition to God to *live in His peace* when you present [or hand over] your requests to Him…even if He doesn't change your circumstances, *seek His peace*." (paraphrased from *Owned* sermon series – Part 3[24]).

"You don't need to know where you are going when you trust in who you are following." (unknown author)

<u>What I Learned or Was Reminded About:</u>

- My darkness in the desert is a season – don't forget that!
- Wait on the Lord - not the answer - because the answer is not as important as the Lord.
- G_d's peace can carry me through anything.

<u>What I Prayed:</u>

Lord – I have very little "light" in my life during this desert season. Direct sunlight does not even come into my apartment very often. I miss direct sun rays – for I've always felt closest to you when the sun is basking on my face. I have no direction…no light…for my career path, which is the income I need to move out of my desert into the next stage of my life. My "petition" is to buy a house with a yard in order to get my dogs back. I long for that to happen as I continue to sit on your lap in peace, trusting in your timing.

============================

10/7/Sun (late day)

What G_d Said:

"Abram *believed the Lord,* and he credited it to him as righteousness." (Genesis 15:6).

What I Learned or Was Reminded About:

- G_d's character will never let Him lie or deceive me. I should always believe what He says, because it will always come to pass.

What I Prayed:

Lord – During my Torah Club study I literally had a thought cross my mind that only you could've spoken to me. At the moment I heard it, I was angry at what I sensed you said "might" happen. Tears are streaming down my face in anger!! But alas, what I do know to be true is that you are the God of transformation and you and ONLY you know what is best for me. I want no part of the "might" happen…but I am prepared to submit my will to you - because ultimately your plan is always better than mine.

Abraham stepped out in faith without knowing where you were leading him. I continue to step out in faith not knowing where you are leading me. In the past I've always gone where you've asked me to go - though sometimes I needed to get past the shock of it first, and occasionally work through a bit of a temper tantrum - until I was able to settle more comfortably into your will for my life.

For right now I stand on the word "might" NOT. I cling to the hope that what you said might happen is a test of my submission to you and not a certainty of the situation itself ….though I'm laughing out loud now at how absurd my argument/logical conclusion is – because if I get to a place of content submission, I will ultimately be fine and trusting whether that situation comes to pass or not.

BE CONTENT is the theme of my desert season along with WAIT and SURRENDER. I long to be released into my new life, and petition for that release to occur before 2013. PLEASE Lord, deliver the income quickly so I can get a house to get my dogs back and restore everything I lost this year.

10/8/Mon

What G_d Said:

"...the *joy of the Lord is your strength.*" (Nehemiah 8:10B)

"He has sent me to bind up the brokenhearted, to proclaim freedom for the captives and release from darkness for the prisoners, to *proclaim the year of the Lord's favor* and the day of vengeance of our God, to comfort all who mourn, and provide for those who grieve in Zion - to bestow on them a crown of beauty instead of ashes, the oil of gladness instead of mourning, and a garment of praise instead of a spirit of despair. They will be called oaks of righteousness, *a planting of the Lord for the display of his splendor.*" (Isaiah 61:1B-3)

What I Learned or Was Reminded About:

- The ability to be joyful in my desert comes from G_d, not my own strength.
- I will see the year of the Lord's favor eventually.

What I Prayed:

Lord – I am deepening my ability to submit to your will, be content in my circumstances, and be still and wait on you. I know that joy in you is my strength. I am thankful for all you've provided and especially that I HEAR YOU more clearly through scripture, and occasionally feel you. THANK YOU for that. As always, I await your leading and trust the door to my new career and life will open at the right time.

10/9/Tue

What G_d Said:

"Yet *the Lord longs to be gracious to you*; he rises to show you compassion. For the Lord is the *God of justice*. Blessed are *all who wait for Him*!" (Isaiah 30:18).

"And my God will *meet all your needs* according to his glorious riches in Christ Jesus." (Philippians 4:19)

"*Is anything too hard for the Lord*?" (Genesis 18:14A)

What I Learned or Was Reminded About:

- G_d has always met my needs and will continue to do so. Nothing is too hard for Him!

What I Prayed:

Lord – I am excited about my next career and how you will use me to impact those around me. I continue to wait in my desert season and trust that you will meet all my needs because nothing is impossible for you.

10/10/Wed

What G_d Said:

"…no one can come to me unless the *Father has enabled him*…no one can come to me unless *the Father who sent me draws him*…" (John 6:65 and 6:44A)

"*Before they call I will answer,* while they are still speaking I will hear." (Isaiah 65:24)

What I Learned or Was Reminded About:

- We come into a relationship with G_d because He draws us to Him – our choice is to walk towards or away from Him.
- G_d always knows what I need before I say it.

What I Prayed:

Lord – There are so many people I love that do not have a relationship with you. Thank you for the reminder that YOU must initiate the relationship and enable them to come to you. My guess is that you are "knocking" on their heart, but at this moment they can't or are refusing to acknowledge you.

I ask, Lord, that you keep knocking – but more loudly – and that you soften their mindset, eyes and ears to hear you. Let them become curious enough to investigate the truth of who you are. Give them the courage to listen and open the door of their heart to you, and provide non-threatening and loving believers to help them along the way.

Thank you also for answering my prayers and needs before I even say them.

10/19/Fri & 10/20/Sat [Dog Sitting Weekend!! ☺]

<u>What G_d Said:</u>

"For none of us lives to himself alone and none of us dies to himself alone. If we live, we live to the Lord; and if we die, we die to the Lord. *So whether we live or die, we belong to the Lord*." (Romans 14:7-8)

"*I wait for you*, O Lord; You will answer, O Lord my God." (Psalm 38:15)

"*For where your treasure is, there your heart will be also*." (Matthew 6:21)

<u>What I Learned or Was Reminded About:</u>

- This world is temporary, and I am capable of waiting through any circumstance.

<u>What I Prayed:</u>

Lord – I know I belong to you, and because of that I continue to wait for you. My treasure is YOU; therefore, my heart is full of you.

Thank you for Danny giving me the weekend to dog-sit my girls at the house while he is in Florida. It's been such a blessing to revel in all the sunlight and privacy I've missed so much at my apartment. I continue to wait for a new job to get the house with a yard which will finally allow me to get my girls back full-time.

10/21/Sun

<u>What G_d Said:</u>

"*This is the day the Lord has made*; let us rejoice and be glad in it." (Psalm 118:24)

"Show me your ways, O Lord, *teach me your paths; guide me in your truth* and teach me, for you are God my Savior, and my hope is in you all day long" (Psalm 25:4-5)

"…If anyone would come after me, he must deny himself and take up his cross and follow me. For whoever loses his life for me will find it." (Matthew 16:24-25)

"Do not be like them, for *your Father knows what you need before you ask him.*" (Matthew 6:8)

"*Ask and it will be given to you*; seek and you will find; knock and the door will be opened to you. For everyone who asks receives; he who seeks finds; and to him who knocks, the door will be opened." (Matthew 7:7-8)

<u>What I Learned or Was Reminded About:</u>

- Every day is a blessing because I can trust in my G_d who sees my future clearly.

<u>What I Prayed:</u>

Lord – Thank you for the reminder that every day I have breath is a day I should rejoice in you – no matter what is going on in my life. Thank you for the wonderful weekend with my girls, even though I have to go back to my apartment tomorrow. I'm glad you are in my life working behind the scenes to set up my future and provide for me.

10/22/Mon & 10/23/Tue

What G_d Said:

"Know that the Lord has set apart the godly for himself; *the Lord will hear when I call to him.*" (Psalm 4:3)

"*Be still and know I am God...*" (Psalm 46:10)

"I have told you these things, so that *in me you may have peace*. In this world *you will have trouble*. But take heart! I have overcome the world." (John 16:33)

> "Therefore, instead of analyzing our problems and trying to figure out a solution, let's start with trying to see God...Instead of learning as much as possible about the situation, learn what God says about it." (*Learning to Live Above* / "Secret of Knowing" p 123-124)

What I Learned or Was Reminded About:

- Troubles will always find their way to me. If I focus on G_d, I will have peace to journey through them.

What I Prayed:

Lord- Thank you for the reminder to focus on you first (on what you may be saying or how you are directing me), rather than me spending my energy trying to solve a difficult circumstance. I know you have "overcome the world" and so there is no need for me to worry about anything.

Thank you again for the gift of being with my furry children all weekend, and for the sunshine so I could lie on the lawn, read books, and revel in the privacy I've missed while in my apartment. I look forward to seeing you restore all that I've lost and trust in you completely.

10/24/Wed

What G_d Said:

"Come to me, all you who are weary and burdened, and *I will give you rest.*" (Matthew 11:28)

"'For my thoughts are not your thoughts, neither are your ways my ways,' declares the Lord. 'As the heavens are higher than the earth, so are *my ways higher than your ways, and my thoughts higher than your thoughts.*" (Isaiah 55:8-9)

"Many are the plans in a man's heart, but it is *the Lord's purpose that prevails.*" (Proverbs 19:21)

"But God has revealed it to us by His Spirit…*no one knows the thoughts of God except the Spirit of God*…The man without the Spirit does not accept the things that come from the Spirit of God, for they are foolishness to him, and he cannot understand them, because *they are spiritually discerned*. The spiritual man makes judgments about all things, but he himself is not subject to any man's judgment: 'For who has known the mind of the Lord that he may instruct him?' *But we have the mind of Christ.*" (1 Corinthians 2:10A, 11B, and 14-16)

"But when he, the Spirit of truth, comes, *he will guide you into all truth*. He will not speak on his own; he will speak only what he hears, and he will tell you what is yet to come." (John 16:13)

What I Learned or Was Reminded About:

- Only in G_d do I have true rest.
- Spiritual things can only be understood by those who have the Spirit of G_d within them.

What I Prayed:

Lord – Thank you for all the verses you gave me today. As I move forward, help me to discern what you say to me in your Word through your confirmation in my prayers, circumstances, and the counsel of other believers.

10/25/Thu

<u>What G_d Said:</u>

"*Stop trusting in man*, who has but a breath in his nostrils. Of what account is he?" (Isaiah 2:22)

"If the Lord delights in a man's way, *he makes his steps firm*; though he stumble, he will not fall, for the Lord upholds him with his hand." (Psalm 37:23-24)

"*Commit to the Lord whatever you do*, and your plans will succeed." (Proverbs 16:3)

"For it is God who works in you *to will and to act according to his good purpose.*" (Philippians 2:13)

<u>What I Learned or Was Reminded About:</u>

- G_d will make my steps firm if I commit what I do to Him and if it is according to His purpose.

<u>What I Prayed:</u>

Lord – Thank you for making my steps firm because I have submitted my will to you with regards to my future. You know I have committed my actions to you every step of my journey and look forward to seeing the door out of my desert appear in your perfect time.

10/26/Fri

<u>What G_d Said:</u>

"Do not conform any longer to the pattern of this world, but *be transformed by the renewing of your mind*. Then you will be able to *test and approve what God's will is* – his good, pleasing and perfect will." (Romans 12:2)

<u>What I Learned or Was Reminded About:</u>

- It's not about me...it's about who G_d is transforming me into!

<u>What I Prayed:</u>

Lord – I am starting to get really annoyed at the length of my desert season. I'm tired of working as a Server at Taco Mac, and so badly want to move on to a job I love.

I continue to submit my will to you and ask that you release me before the end of the year. I remain content to be in the palm of your hand, yet the human part of me longs for more. Keep transforming and renewing my mind so I can stay at peace in this desert season.

10/27/Sat

What G d Said:

"Are not five sparrows sold for two pennies? *Yet not one of them is forgotten by God.* Indeed, the very hairs of your head are all numbered. *Don't be afraid; you are worth more than many sparrows.*" (Luke 12:6-7)

"Deep calls to deep in the roar of your waterfalls; all your waves and breakers have swept over me. By day the Lord directs his love, at night his song is with me – a prayer to the God of my life…*Put your hope in God*, for I will yet *praise Him*, my Savior and my God." (Psalm 42:7-8, 11B)

> "*They are HIS waves*, whether for our comfort…or to our cry there comes *no aid or answer, and* in the *lonely silence* none is near…They are HIS waves, whether he *separates them…or let's tumultuous breakers surge about us*…They are HIS waves, and *He directs us through them*; So He has promised, so His love will do. *Keeping and leading, guiding and upholding, to His sure harbor, He will bring us through.*" (Poem by Ann Johnson Flint from *Streams in the Desert*, 10/27 commentary)

"*Finally, be strong in the Lord and in his mighty power. Put on the full armor of God* so that you can take your stand against the devil's schemes. For our struggle is not against flesh and blood, but against the rulers, against the authorities, against the powers of this dark world and against the spiritual forces of evil in the heavenly realms. Therefore put on the full armor of God, so that when the day of evil comes, you may be able to stand your ground, and after you have done everything, to stand. *Stand firm then with*

- *the belt of truth* buckled around your waist, with
- *the breastplate of righteousness* in place, and with your
- *feet fitted with readiness* that comes from the gospel of peace. In addition to all this, take up the

- *shield of faith*, with which you can extinguish all the flaming arrows of the evil one. Take the
- *helmet of salvation* and the
- *sword of the Spirit* which is the word of God

And pray in the Spirit on all occasions with all kinds of prayers and requests. With this in mind, *be alert* and always keep on praying for all the saints." (Ephesians 6:10-18)

"…Do not be afraid, Abram, *I am your shield*, your very great reward!" (Genesis 15:1B)

What I Learned or Was Reminded About:

- G_d will never forget me, no matter how lost I feel at times. He is my shield and through Christ I have a full armor of G_d in which to stand firm in any circumstance.

What I Prayed:

Lord – Thank you for being my shield so that I am able to maneuver through my desert with a deep sense of peace, despite the weariness and frustration I feel. I continue to be still and wait on you, and maintain my contentment regardless of my circumstances.

10/28/Sun

<u>What G_d Said:</u>

"And God raised us up with Christ and *seated us with him* in the heavenly realms in Christ Jesus, in order that in the coming ages he might show the incomparable riches of his grace, expressed in his kindness to us in Christ Jesus." (Ephesians 2:6-7)

<u>What I Learned or Was Reminded About:</u>

- Through seating us with Him, G_d allows us the luxury of being still and trusting Him as He continues to work on our behalf.

<u>What I Prayed:</u>

Lord – Thank you for the continual reminder, when my natural tendency to "do something" kicks in, to remember you want me to BE STILL, and NOT strive…but rather to rest assured you are at work behind the scenes even though I can't see it right now.

My desert is a season, not a life sentence, and you will deliver me from it when the timing is right so you can restore your blessings to me in your way – which is perfect. I love and trust you during this time, and will not let it go wasted by continuing to delve into your Word and your peace.

Be Still? Really, Lord??

10/29/Mon

What G_d Said:

"But you must *return to your God*; maintain love and justice, and *wait for your God always.*" (Hosea 12:6)

"He will sit as a refiner and purifier of silver…" (Malachi 3:3A)

"…Do not *interpretations belong to God*?…" (Genesis 40:8B)

"Flesh gives birth to flesh, but the *Spirit gives birth to spirit.*" (John 3:6)

"God is spirit and *his worshippers must worship in spirit and in truth.*" (John 4:24)

"Whatever you do, *work at it with all your heart, as working for the Lord, not for men*, since you know that you will receive an inheritance from the Lord as a reward. It is the Lord Christ you are serving." (Colossians 3:23-24)

"But if you suffer for doing good and you endure it, this is commendable before God. To this you were called, because Christ suffered for you, leaving *you an example, that you should follow in his steps.*" (1 Peter 2:20B-21)

What I Learned or Was Reminded About:

- Just as a metal refiner sits next to the kiln to ensure the metal does not suffer more heat than necessary in order to remove the dross (impurities removed from metal), G_d sits with us during our trials. If we wait for Him to refine us as He wishes, we'll always turn out exactly as He planned.
- Only G_d can truly interpret a circumstance perfectly.
- Always do everything with full effort and integrity as though G_d asked you to do it Himself.
- My actions are always a reflection of Jesus within me, therefore I should always be careful to represent Him well.

What I Prayed:

Lord – I laughed when I saw the *Wisdom Hunters* devotional titled, "Chosen to Wait" in my Inbox this morning. I love how you continue to gently remind me to be still and wait on you whenever my DNA driven nature starts to get frustrated.

Thank you for using this desert season to refine me, and remove the "dross" from my life. I trust that you will release me from my desert not a second late (though "early" would be preferable!).

10/30/Tue

<u>What G_d Said:</u>

"The unfolding of your words gives light; *it gives understanding* to the simple." (Psalm 119:130)

"The Lord will fight for you; *you need only to be still.*" (Exodus 14:14)

<u>What I Learned or Was Reminded About:</u>

- Your Word provides understanding when I do not understand.
- When I am still, I won't interfere with G_d's work behind the scenes.

<u>What I Prayed:</u>

Lord – Thank you for continuing to speak to me through your Word which sheds "light" on how I am to handle my desert season. I "understand" and trust that you are "fighting for me" behind the scenes. My job is to BE STILL.

I miss being active in a leadership position - using my skills and talents to encourage and develop others - and making things happen through my business/career. However, I know you have me "still" for a reason, and I honor your decision. I wait contently, knowing you will release me not a moment later than necessary.

10/31/Wed

What G_d Said:

"*But if we hope for what we do not yet have, we wait for it patiently.* In the same way, the Spirit helps us in our weakness. We do not know what we ought to pray for, but the Spirit himself intercedes for us with groans that words cannot express. And he who searches our hearts knows the mind of the Spirit, because the Spirit intercedes for the saints in accordance with God's will. And we know that in all things *God works for the good of those who love him*, who have been called according to his purpose." (Romans 8:25-28)

"Now faith is being sure of what we hope for and certain of what we do not see…And *without faith it is impossible to please God*, because anyone who comes to him must believe that he exists and that he rewards those who earnestly seek Him….All these people were still living by faith when they died. They did not receive the things promised; they only saw them and welcomed them from a distance. And they *admitted that they were aliens and strangers on earth*." (Hebrews 11:1, 6, and 13)

"*These were all commended for their faith*, yet none of them received what had been promised. God had planned something better for us so that only together with us would they be made perfect." (Hebrews 11:39-40)

What I Learned or Was Reminded About:

- Consequences of being a faithful believer can be either: a) victory and deliverance (Hebrews 11:33-35A) or b) torture, mockery, or death (Hebrews 35B-38). If I believe G_d is my Lord and has me in the palm of His hand, I should be content to walk in any of those circumstances and have faith that G_d will use me for His glory.

What I Prayed:

I actually forgot to write down my prayer this day. But, what I do remember about it is that it was the first time I began to feel a deep awareness that my perception of my life on this earth was changing.

Be Still? Really, Lord??

My desert journey had begun to bear amazing fruit: No longer was I focused on the blessings I would receive or the happiness I would eventually experience during my lifetime - Hebrews 11:32-40 made it clear that God could call me to torture, mockery or death as easily as victory and deliverance.

A light bulb went on when I realized I could be released from my desert season into even more difficult circumstances - because nowhere in scripture does G_d promise anyone "good times." I knew that I had to begin to look beyond myself and be willing to walk into a season of torture, mockery or death if G_d called me into it.

Was I willing? That question followed me around all day. I wanted to say "yes" - but was I really? For months I had been begging G_d to give me an income to buy a house to get my dogs back. What if that was NOT the future He had in mind for me? Would I praise Him anyway? Would I give Him the honor and respect, the love and trust He deserves if He chose NOT to restore what I lost?

If He is my Lord, the answer has to be YES! If He is my Lord, I must follow whatever path He sets before me because I know my earthly life is temporary – just a stop over until I reach eternity in heaven.

All that day I realized G_d was truly PRESSING into me that I need to stop focusing on my wants on this earth and instead focus on being of service to Him, even if torture, mockery and death are the result.

As the day went on, I felt a distinct awareness of my humanity and my spirituality at war within me. Being human, I will never be free of my desire for "good times", nor do I believe God wants me to be free of it (because He loves to give His children their heart's desire [Psalm 37:4]). What I think He was asking of me this day is *would I be willing to lay them aside if He asked me to*?

The answer is…ABSOLUTELY YES, with His help!

11/1/Thu

<u>What G_d Said:</u>

"*I waited patiently for the Lord*; he turned to me and heard my cry…You are my help and *my deliverer, O my God, do not delay.*" (Psalm 40:1, 17B)

"*Who of you by worrying can add a single hour to his life*? Since you cannot do this very little thing, why do you worry about the rest?" (Luke 12:25-26)

<u>What I Learned or Was Reminded About:</u>

- If I am obeying G_d through waiting patiently, He expects to occasionally hear my human cries and my requests asking Him not to delay in delivering me from my circumstances (I am human after all!!). My job is to be content with His answer, no matter what it is.

<u>What I Prayed:</u>

Lord – Tomorrow would be my 10th anniversary. Instead it is the 10th month since Danny told me he wanted to move forward with the divorce. I moved out in April, which makes tomorrow the 8th month of my being in this desert. I am tired of being on hold and have very little to do except wait.

"Oh, G_d, do not delay" my release from my desert any longer than you have to! I want to SEE what is on the other side of the door to my future. I ask for that view, however you want to deliver that knowledge. Please let me see it and know without a doubt that IT is my future no matter what it is…because you know I will always submit to your will – even if I'm not initially happy about it.

Thank you for the continuous provision and protection you provide, and the support and encouragement from others as I continue to be still and wait on you; content to be in the palm of your hand during my desert season.

11/3/Sat

<u>What G_d Said:</u>

"Those who know your name *will trust in you*, for you, Lord, have *never forsaken* those who seek you." (Psalm 9:10)

<u>What I Learned or Was Reminded About:</u>

- G_d will never forsake me!

<u>What I Prayed:</u>

Lord – I do trust in you and know you will never forsake me. Please keep my spiritual eyes and ears extra attentive to your leading while I am in this desert season.

11/5/Mon

<u>What G_d Said:</u>

"Humble yourselves, therefore, under God's mighty hand, that *He may lift you up in due time. Cast all your anxiety on him* because he cares for you." (1 Peter 5:6-7)

"I will say of the Lord, 'He is my refuge and my fortress, my God, in whom I trust….'Because he loves me,' says the Lord, 'I will rescue him; I will protect him, for he acknowledges my name. He will call upon me and I will answer him; I will be with him in trouble, I will *deliver him and honor him*. With long life I will satisfy him, and show him my salvation." (Psalm 91:2, 14-16)

<u>What I Learned or Was Reminded About:</u>

- G_d will always deliver me - even at the extreme of death (that is certainly one delivery avenue!), therefore I must honor him in all circumstances.

<u>What I Prayed:</u>

Lord – I do humble myself before you and look forward to when you will "lift me up" out of my desert. Until then, I "cast all my anxiety on you" and know you are my "refuge and fortress."

11/6/Tue & 11/7/Wed

What G_d Said:

"...any of you who does not *give up everything he has* cannot be my disciple." (Luke 14:33)

"...the Father judges no one, but has entrusted all judgment to the Son, that all may honor the Son just as they honor the Father. *He who does not honor the Son does not honor the Father*, who sent him." (John 5:22-23)

"You will keep *in perfect peace* him whose mind is steadfast, *because he trusts in you*. Trust in the Lord forever, for the Lord, the Lord, is the Rock eternal." (Isaiah 26:3-4)

"While I'm Waiting"[25] - lyrics from a song by John Waller, sent to me by one of the ladies in my Bible Study group.

What I Learned or Was Reminded About:

- I must be willing to give up everything for G_d if He asks - otherwise I am not honoring Him.
- Perfect peace is available in G_d when I trust in Him.

What I Prayed:

Lord – I am focusing on surrendering everything over to you. I know my life is in your hands and you will bring good out of every circumstance as long as I have breath in my body...and beyond that.

11/9/Fri

What G_d Said:

"These are the words of him who is holy and true, who holds the key of David. *What he opens no one can shut, and what he shuts no one can open.* I know your deeds. See, *I have placed before you an open door that no one can shut.* I know that you have little strength, yet *you have kept my word and not denied my name.*" (Revelations 3:7B-8)

"So do not fear, for I am with you; *do not be dismayed*, for I am your God. *I will strengthen you and help you*; I will uphold you with my righteous right hand." (Isaiah 41:10)

"I will make known the end from the beginning, from ancient times, what is still to come. I say: *My purpose will stand*, and I do all that I please. From the east I summon a bird of prey; from a far-off land, a man to fulfill my purpose. *What I have said, that I will bring about*; what I have planned, that I will do." (Isaiah 46:10-11)

"In the morning, O Lord, *you hear my voice*; in the morning I lay my requests before you and *wait in expectation*." (Psalm 5:3)

What I Learned or Was Reminded About:

- G_d's purposes will ALWAYS come to pass, even if we screw it up along the way – so it's always best to wait in expectation and lean on G_d's strength each step of the way.

What I Prayed:

Lord – My desert season continues. The benefit is that I have time to spend with you in your Word...and I'm thrilled I now have direct sunlight by which to read because of winter sky changes (THANK YOU FOR THAT!).

I am tired of waiting, but am constantly reminded by your Word of what you want from me and who you are:

- ◊ "I have placed before you an open door that no one can shut"
    - a. I declare the door exists even though I can't see it.
- ◊ "Do not be dismayed"
    - a. I declare that I will stand in my faith, and not in my feelings.
- ◊ "My purpose will stand"
    - a. I declare your purpose for the next season of my life will arrive in your perfect timing.
- ◊ "You hear my voice"
    - a. I declare my prayers are heard and addressed, and I will continue to "wait in expectation" of your answer.

I stand in two worlds: spiritual trust and human feeling…bouncing from one to the other. Thank you for all the previous faith-building circumstances in my life that have prepared me for this moment and time, allowing me to lean more on the spiritual side.

I expectantly wait for you to release me from my desert, and can't wait to see what that looks like.

11/10/Sat

What G_d Said:

"*Against all hope, Abraham in hope believed* and so became the father of many nations, just as it had been said to him, 'So shall your offspring be.'" (Romans 4:18)

> "He [God] generally waits to send his help until the time of our greatest need, *so that His hand will be plainly seen in our deliverance*..." (*Streams in the Desert*, 11/10 commentary)

"O Lord, *you have searched me and you know me...Before a word is on my tongue you know it completely*, O Lord...Where can I go from your Spirit? Where can I flee from your presence?...For you created my inmost being; you knit me together in my mother's womb. I praise you because I am fearfully and wonderfully made; your works are wonderful. I know that full well...All the days ordained for me were written in your book before one of them came to be. *How precious to me are your thoughts, O God!* How vast is the sum of them!" (Psalm 139:1, 4, 7, 13-14, and 16B-17)

What I Learned or Was Reminded About:

- When we gain confirmation about what G_d is saying to us, we need to believe "against all hope" it will come to pass, even if it's a lifetime.
- You know my innermost thoughts, so it's best to always be honest with you, especially when I know I am coming up short.

What I Prayed:

Lord – Like Abraham, our greatest example of a faith-lived lifetime, I believe you will provide what I need, when I need it and I have great hope you will restore all that I lost this year. You have "searched me and know me," and know everything before I say or do it. Your thoughts are precious to me. I long to receive your guidance about how to move forward, and yet I trust that you also have a purpose for my being still and waiting. I look forward to celebrating when my desert release occurs.

11/11/Sun

What G_d Said:

"...for I have *learned to be content* whatever the circumstances" (Philippians 4:11B)

"*Give thanks to the Lord, call on his name; make known among the nations what he has done.* Sing to him, sing praise to him; *tell of all his wondrous acts.* Glory in his holy name; let the hearts of those who seek the Lord rejoice. Look to the Lord and his strength; seek his face always. Remember the wonders he has done, his miracles, and the judgments he pronounced." (1 Chronicles 16:8-12)

What I Learned or Was Reminded About:

- I need to let go of my feelings and just be content to sit in my circumstances until G_d releases me.
- Sharing my story with my personal and professional network over the last few months about how G_d is using my desert season to deepen and widen my faith has become a living testimony "of all his wondrous acts."

What I Prayed:

Lord – Your will for my life is what is best for me in the long run. I don't want to go without the things I want (high income, house, dogs), but I also know surrender to you is more important to me than material desires.

This world is temporary – in my heart I live for the eternal place you've promised me in Heaven. My head logically knows this, but my heart wants earthly happiness too.

There is nothing wrong with having both (there are plenty of faithful believers you have blessed with wealth and other material things) – but having it at the expense of walking outside your will is not worth it to me. Let me know your thoughts and guide me quickly out of my desert into the "promised land" you have laid aside for me on this earth and in heaven.

11/13/Tue

<u>What G_d Said:</u>

"Naked I came from my mother's womb, and naked I will depart. *The Lord gave and the Lord has taken away; may the name of the Lord be praised.*" (Job 1:21)

"Now listen, you who say, 'Today or tomorrow we will go to this or that city, spend a year there, carry on business and make money.' Why, you do not even know what will happen tomorrow. What is your life? *You are a mist that appears for a while then vanishes.* Instead you ought to say, '*If it is the Lord's will* we will live and do this or that." (James 4:13-15)

"Because of the Lord's great love we are not consumed, for his compassions never fail. They are new every morning; great is your faithfulness. I say to myself, 'The Lord is my portion; *therefore I will wait for him.*' The Lord is good to those whose hope is in him, to the one who seeks him." (Lamentations 3:22-25)

<u>What I Learned or Was Reminded About:</u>

- Job, a faithful believer, lost everything and still praised the name of the Lord. Why should I do any differently?

<u>What I Prayed:</u>

Lord – Over my lifetime you have given me far more than you have taken – though the "taken" always hurts deeply (and sometimes it is not even you doing the taking…it's me running ahead of you or other people's free will interfering with the plans you have for me).

When you do "take", I know you see the bigger picture, and give and take based on that knowledge <u>because</u> you know my needs.

I am just a "mist that appears for a while than vanishes." In the big scheme of things, my life on this earth is just a stopover. Heaven is my eternal home.

I continue to become comfortable with my new depth of understanding around "if it is the Lord's will, we will live and do this or that." I must remember that today is temporary and my heart and soul, feelings and desires all need to be focused primarily on my heavenly destination…even if I am here on earth a long time.

11/15/Thu

<u>What G_d Said:</u>

"*Keep on doing the things that you have learned* and received and heard and seen in me, and the *God of peace will be with you.*" (Philippians 4:9, Revised Standard Version translation)

<u>What I Learned or Was Reminded About:</u>

- In times of uncertainty, I must keep doing what I've learned in order to remain secure underneath the umbrella of G_d's peace as I continue forward with my life - despite that uncertainty.

<u>What I Prayed:</u>

Lord - Thank you for all the things I've learned, received, heard, and seen from you since February. Thank you for your peace and for all the amazing people you've put into my life to support and encourage me through my journey into an unknown future.

11/16/Fri

What G_d Said:

"*Unless the Lord builds the house*, its builders labor in vain. *Unless the Lord watches* over the city, the watchmen stand guard in vain. In vain you rise early and stay up late, *toiling for food to eat* – for he grants sleep to those he loves." (Psalm 127:1-2)

"*…My grace is sufficient for you, for my power is made perfect in weakness.*" (2 Corinthians 12:9A)

What I Learned or Was Reminded About:

- If I do not include G_d in my plans, I toil in vain. I'd rather consult Him so I can "sleep" (be at peace) more easily.

What I Prayed:

I forgot to write a prayer on this day. However, had I done so, I would have written this:

Lord – I know from 44 years of making important decisions that anytime I ran ahead without consulting you, I tended to fall flat on my face. I do not like "toiling in vain." I have truly learned that when I consult you and wait for your answer I am more at peace and "sleep" more easily.

I took a look at my checkbook today and my heart started to race because I am at that point when I can actually calculate when the money will run out if you do not provide another source of income.

Logically it still doesn't make sense that you want me to remain still and wait on you to deliver a job instead of me running around (toiling) trying to make it happen under my own power. But spiritually, I truly feel you asking me to trust you, and many of the scriptures you've delivered over the last few weeks have confirmed that.

Could I be wrong? Sure – it's possible. But I've learned to trust my gut when scripture aligns with what I feel to be true. And besides, what is the worst thing that will happen if I'm wrong? I'll have to move and figure out how to survive from there. Do I like that scenario – absolutely not! Do I trust that you'll be with me, absolutely!

Your "grace is sufficient for me", and I know your "power is made perfect in weakness." So I humbly walk forward in faith that you will deliver the job before the money runs out, and know that if it doesn't happen – you will provide another path for me to take.

Yes, I'm nervous. But I'm also at peace.

Yes, I'm frustrated. But I'm also secure in you.

Yes, I'm tired. But I'm also excited about my future.

Keep me focused on you and your promises as my checkbook balance continues to drop. Let me stand firmly on the knowledge that as long as I seek your will, you will provide me the strength to get through any challenges or anxieties I may face.

11/16/Sat

What G_d Said:

"For we know him who said, '*It is mine to avenge*; I will repay,' and again, 'The Lord will judge his people.' It is a dreadful thing to fall in the hands of the living God." (Hebrews 10:30-31)

"These [all of creation] look to you to g*ive them their food at the proper time*. When you give it to them, they gather it up; when you open your hand, they are satisfied with good things. When you hide your face, they are terrified; when you take away their breath, they die and return to the dust. When you send your Spirit they are created, and you renew the face of the earth…*May my meditation be pleasing to him; as I rejoice in the Lord*." (Psalm 104: 27-30, and 34)

"Then Jesus told his disciples a parable to show them *they should always pray and not give up*. He said: 'In a certain town there was a judge who neither feared God nor cared about men. And there was a widow in that town who kept coming to him with the plea, 'Grant me justice against my adversary.' For some time he refused. But finally he said to himself, 'Even though I don't fear God or care about men, yet because this widow keeps bothering me, I will see she gets justice, so that she won't eventually wear me out with her coming!' And the Lord said, 'Listen to what the unjust judge says. And will not God bring about justice for his chosen ones, who cry out to him day and night? Will he keep putting them off? I tell you, *he will see that they get justice, and quickly*." (Luke 18:1-8A)

What I Learned or Was Reminded About:

- After I have addressed a wrong, if I still feel a lack of justice and the other person refuses to give me what I need to make it right…I must then leave that person in G_d's hands, trusting He will be just in how He deals with him/her.

- You always provide what we need at "the proper time." May I default to rejoicing in you, regardless of whether my needs are met.
- I should never cease praying and not give up. As long as I am willing to submit to your will in everything and delight in you, you long to grant my heart's desires.(Psalm 37:4)

What I Prayed:

Lord – I woke up this morning with the memory of the words of a conversation from the past that has been the source of much hurt and unanswered questions for many years. Before even getting out of bed I remember thinking, "I hope someday that person apologizes and has a deep enlightened awareness of how those words and actions really impacted our lives." So I know it isn't just coincidence that two of the three scriptures you gave me this morning through my devotions were about your justice system.

I recognize forgiveness is a process of doing it over and over again, because I have forgiven this situation before (and actually forgotten it for a while too). Yet every now and then the wound speaks softly to me – wanting justice and the truth as I understand it to be shouted from the mountaintops. I may never know why things happened the way they did, but I must trust YOU do, and that you will either deliver justice or mercy as you see fit.

11/18/Sun

<u>What G_d Said:</u>

"As the rain and the snow come down from heaven, and do not return to it without watering the earth and making it bud and flourish, so that it yields seed for the sower and bread for the eater, *so is my word that goes out from my mouth; It will not return to me empty*, but will accomplish what I desire and achieve the purpose for which I sent it. You will go out in joy and be led forth in peace…This will be for the Lord's renown, for an everlasting sign, which will not be destroyed." (Isaiah 55:10-12A and 13B)

"Oh *the depths of the riches of the wisdom and knowledge of God*!" (Romans 11:33A)

"Command those who are rich in this present world not to be arrogant *nor put their hope in wealth, which is so uncertain*, but to put their hope in *God, who richly provides us with everything for our enjoyment*. Command them to do good, to be rich in good deeds, and to be generous and willing to share. In this way they will lay up treasure for themselves as a firm foundation for the coming age, so that they *may take hold of the life that is truly life*." (1Timothy 6:17-19)

<u>What I Learned or Was Reminded About:</u>

- There are no riches greater than G_d's wisdom and knowledge.
- True life is not found in material riches, but hope in G_d,

<u>What I Prayed:</u>

Lord – I know your Word "will not return to me empty." After 20+ years of spending time in your Word I am finally sensing the intimacy I've been praying for over the last year. Now, I expect to hear from you and am excited to sit down with my pen and paper to record the guidance you give me through my devotions, sermons, and other people's words. My faith has taken a deep dive to a new richness with you to receive "the depths of the riches in wisdom and knowledge" of you - Thank you for that!

You know I have been asking you for a high-income position, but after listening to Andy Stanley's "Be Rich- Part 2[26]" sermon series this morning, I realize I am really asking you for wealth to help me feel secure financially.

I know what income I think I need financially to purchase a house in Dunwoody with a backyard to bring my girls home to me; but words from a dear friend said months ago keep popping into my head, "Why are you limiting God, Kris? Isn't He capable of providing you a home and yard through other circumstances than just money?"

It seems, once again, I am guilty of trying to "build my own house" (Psalm 127:1) and trying to plan my security. Only you know what will happen tomorrow and how it should happen (James 4:13-15).

I continue to pray for restoration because of your directive in Luke 18:1A to "pray and not give up." I must surrender and trust that restoration in my eyes may be completely different from restoration in your eyes.

Living in uncertainty is the best faith-training experience one can have. As I continue to live in this place, I will continue to practice focusing on you any time my frustration or anxiety appears.

11/19/Mon

<u>What G_d Said:</u>

"Though *you have made me see troubles, many and bitter, you will restore my life again*; from the depths of the earth you will again bring me up. You will *increase my honor* and comfort me once again." (Psalm 71:20-21)

<u>What I Learned or Was Reminded About:</u>

- Restoration will come…expect it and trust it will be delivered exactly as I need to receive it.

<u>What I Prayed:</u>

Lord – Restoration is what I long for. I can't believe it's almost the end of 2012 and often I felt like this year would never end. I am hoping you will choose to open the door to my new life before December 31st so that I can start 2013 fully restored and moving forward with my new life.

This year I have seen my share of "troubles, many and bitter," but have found joy in seeing good come out of it during my desert season.

I know for sure that you purposely denied my business profitability all those years because you knew the divorce was going to happen, and needed to make sure I had absolutely NO financial security in order to make me fully dependent on you during this time in order to grow deeper in my faith to the level it has reached.

Thank you for those troubles, and may your grace give me strength to continue my desert journey for as long as it takes.

11/21/Wed

<u>What G_d Said:</u>

"The law of the Lord is perfect, reviving the soul. The *statutes of the Lord are trustworthy*, making wise the simple. The precepts of the Lord are right, giving joy to the heart. The commands of the Lord are radiant, giving light to the eyes. The fear of the Lord is pure, enduring forever. The ordinances of the Lord are sure and altogether righteous. *They are more precious than gold*, than much pure gold; *they are sweeter than honey*, than honey from the comb. By them is your servant warned; *in keeping them there is great reward* (Psalm 19:7-11)

"Delight in yourself in the Lord and *He will give you the desires of your heart…Be still before the Lord and wait patiently for Him.*" (Psalm 37:4 and 7A)

<u>What I Learned or Was Reminded About:</u>

- Even though sometimes I don't understand why G_d asks me to do something a certain way or be a certain way based on scripture, I know He has a purpose and I trust Him to follow it.

<u>What I Prayed:</u>

Lord – Too many people interpret your Word as a bunch of rules. I often think that's why many people choose "spirituality" over any form of organized religion…they just don't like the "rules."

Your Word (scripture) is not about delivering judgment and rules – it's about providing basic guidelines for living on this earth. Those guidelines are for my well-being and the well-being of others. I don't have to like them all, but I know they have a purpose.

I'm thankful for those guidelines, and even if I don't understand them, I know there is "great reward" in following them.

11/22/Thu (Thanksgiving)

What G_d Said:

"I am the Lord, the God of all mankind. *Is anything too hard for me?*" (Jeremiah 32:27)

"*Be careful that you do not forget the Lord your God, failing to observe his commands, his laws and his decrees that I am giving you this day.* Otherwise when you eat and are satisfied, when you build fine houses and settle down, and when you herds and flocks grow large and your silver and gold increase, and all you have I multiplied, then your heart will become proud and you will forget the Lord your God who brought you out of Egypt, out of the land of slavery…You may say to yourself, 'My power and the strength of my hands have produced this wealth for me.' But *remember the Lord your God, for it is he who gives you the ability to produce wealth, and so confirms his covenant, which he swore to your forefathers, as it is today.*" (Deuteronomy 8:11-14, 17-18)

What I Learned or Was Reminded About:

- My G_d can make anything happen, against all odds
- Everything I have comes from G_d. He can give or take it away whenever He chooses for any reason.

What I Prayed:

Lord – I have never been under the delusion that any of the money or possessions I have (or had in the past) came from me. It always came from you either through the talents or intuition you gave me or though circumstances you organized to deliver them.

I thank you for the years you provided good and steady income to enable me to pay off debts and purchase things I wanted. I thank you for "God moments" you coordinated when your provisions around a situation showed up at just the right time.

You've always taken care of me and now – in my desert season of loss and financial insecurity – you will continue to take care of me again.

Thank you for being my Advocate, my Alpha & Omega, my Bread of Life, my Bridegroom, my Comforter, my Cornerstone, my Deliverer, my High Priest, my King of Kings, my Light of the World, my Master, my Mediator, my Redeemer, my Rock, my Teacher, my Truth, my Shield, and my Counselor.

Without you I am nothing, and with you I can journey through any situation. Thank you for walking beside me and preparing what's ahead of me even though I can't see it.

11/24/Sat

What G_d Said:

"*How long, O Lord*? Will you forget me forever? How long will you hide your face from me?...But I trust in your unfailing love; my heart rejoices in your salvation. *I will sing to the Lord, for he has been good to me.*" (Psalm 13:1, 5-6)

"*I will extol the Lord at all times; his praise will always be on my lips*...I sought the Lord *and he answered me*...The angel of the Lord encamps around those who fear him, and he delivers them...The eyes of the Lord are on the righteous and his ears are attentive to their cry...A righteous man may have many troubles, *but the Lord delivers him from them all.*" (Psalm 34:1, 4A, 7, 15, 19)

What I Learned or Was Reminded About:

- Even if I feel as though G_d has forgotten about my prayer requests, He hasn't. I must continue to trust Him and praise Him regardless of how long it takes.

What I Prayed:

Lord – What an interesting Saturday morning! At 8:30 AM during a holiday weekend, right in the middle of my prayer time, I got a call from an old corporate client asking if I would facilitate a goal-setting session. Not only that, but when I mentioned I was heading off to the Messianic Synagogue for Torah Club, she laughed and said she's always felt the Sabbath was supposed to be celebrated on Saturday, and that she studied Hebrew for a while.

The oddity of this phone call from that person at that moment gives me hope that you might be beginning to reveal my future – or at least providing me interim money until my future comes together.

I'm not anxious about my checkbook balance just yet – I'm just really tired of waiting. "How long, Oh Lord? Will you forget me forever?" really spoke to me this morning.

The answer, of course – is NEVER. You will never forget me – that phone call proves it.

As I continue to watch the year come to an end and my checkbook balance drop, help me to manage my impatience and human anxiety about my uncertain future.

I don't want to move back to the frigid north to live with my parents and be too far to visit my girls. However, I am constantly reminded of "not my will, but yours" (Luke 22:42) and must continue to trust that your will is always best. I do trust in you, even though I may not like where I'm heading.

Happier and financially secure times are coming – Lord, I can't wait to live them!

11/25/Sun

<u>What G_d Said:</u>

"The sacrifices of God are *a broken spirit*; a broken and *contrite heart*, Oh God, you will not despise." (Psalm 51:17)

> "*Do not be afraid of brokenness*. Invite it as a blessing instead of ignoring it as a burden. Brokenness is God's way to blessing and change. He breaks our will and restores us into the wisdom of his will....Brokenness is our transformation by his grace and truth. God breaks us to conform us into the image of his son." (*Wisdom Hunters* / "Broken by God")

"No one can serve two masters. Either he will hate the one and love the other, or he will be devoted to one and despise the other. *You cannot serve both God and Money.*" (Matthew 6:24)

"And Moses said, 'Here I am'" (Exodus 3:4B)

> In Hebrew "Here I am" comes from the word "Hineni" which means: *I'm here and ready to listen, ready to respond, and ready to obey* (from Torah Club Volume 1, "Shemot," p. 208). This word is also used by Abraham in Genesis 22:1, Jacob in Genesis 31:11 and Isaiah in Isaiah 6:8.

"*My soul waits in silence for God only*; From Him is my salvation. He only is my rock and my salvation; my stronghold; *I shall not be greatly shaken.*" (Psalm 62:1-2, New American Standard Bible)

Then he said, 'Take the arrows' [the Lord's arrows of victory] and the King took them. Elisha told him 'strike the ground.' He struck it three times and stopped. The man of God was angry with him and said, 'You should have struck the ground five or six times, then you would've defeated Aram and completely destroyed it. But now you will defeat it only three times.' (paraphrased from 2 Kings 13:14-20).

"This story doesn't seem fair to me. How was the King supposed to know he should keep striking? I think the point is if God says to hit three times, then you hit it three times. But if God simply says hit it, *you hit it until he says stop!*" (*Intercessory Prayer*[27] by Dutch Sheets, p. 221)

What I Learned or Was Reminded About:

- When I am in a situation that seems to be breaking me, I must trust G_d will bring good out of it in some way – especially if He did not cause the situation to happen.
- When G_d invites me to participate in His work, my answer needs to be pure "Hineni": being willing to listen, respond and obey immediately - and without question.
- It's not up to me to interpret G_d's directions. If He tells me to do something and isn't specific about when I should stop doing it – I should keep doing it until He tells me to stop.

What I Prayed:

Lord – Thank you for all the trials you provided in the past that prepared me for this desert season. You know there was no reason to "break me" this year (thank you for that!) and instead used this time to bring me into a desert place where I could learn to understand the phrase "Hineni" through being still with you.

As long as I am actively seeking your presence, am in a growing relationship with you, and saying "Hineni" when you speak to me, money will never be my master.

Help me to continue to hear you clearly and follow your directions so I don't make assumptions, like the King in 2 Kings 13, which could prevent or delay the blessings you have planned for me.

December 31st is almost here. I accept your will – whatever comes my way.

11/26/Mon

What G_d Said:

"*May the God of hope* fill you with all joy and peace as you trust in him, so that you may overflow with hope by the power of the Holy Spirit" (Romans 15:13)

"Do any of the worthless idols of the nations bring rain? Do the skies themselves send down showers? No, it is you, O Lord our God. *Therefore our hope is in you, for you are the one who does all this.*" (Jeremiah 14:22)

"May our Lord Jesus Christ himself and God our Father who loved us and by his grace *gave us eternal encouragement and good hope*, encourage your hearts and strengthen you in every good deed and word." (2 Thessalonians 2:16-17)

"*If God is for us, who can be against us*? He who did not spare his own Son, but gave him up for us all – *how will he not also, along with him, graciously give us all things*?" (Romans 8:31B-32)

What I Learned or Was Reminded About:

- My hope does not reside in what I can do or how I feel, but rather in my Almighty and all-powerful Lord.

What I Prayed:

Lord – Thank you for being my Hope and that you give us "eternal encouragement and good hope." I know if you are for us, "who can be against us?"

Hope is a key ingredient in times of uncertainty, and I'm glad you've given me optimistic tendencies that allow me to hope in you against all odds.

11/27/Tue

What G_d Said:

"*For nothing is impossible with God.*" (Luke 1:37)

"Lord, who may dwell in your sanctuary? Who may live on your holy hill? He
- Whose walk is blameless and
- Who does what is righteous,
- Who speaks the truth from his heart and
- Has no slander on his tongue,
- Who does his neighbor no wrong and
- Casts no slur on his fellowman,
- Who despises a vile man but
- Honors those who fear the Lord,
- Who keeps his oath even when it hurts, and does not change his mind;
- Who lends his money without interest and
- Does not accept a bribe against the innocent.

He who does these things will never be shaken." (Psalm 15:1-5)

> In *Twerski on Prayer*[28], Rabbi Twerski shows how Moses delivered 613 mitzvos (commandments) of the Torah to us and how King David condensed them into eleven character traits (Psalm 15). He follows up this observation as follows: "One cannot love others if one is selfish and totally absorbed in one's self. Developing the 11 characteristics of Psalm 15 eliminates the barriers to love of others. Only then can a person 'so journey in God's tent and dwell in His Holy Mountain.' Only by developing these traits can one aspire to a lasting bond with God." (p. 41)

What I Learned or Was Reminded About:

- Because nothing is impossible for you, I will never be "shaken."

What I Prayed:

Lord – Thank you for the goal-setting retreat facilitation opportunity you provided at the exact moment I needed it to pay my upcoming business bills. As usual, I am thankful I can laugh in amusement at your waiting until I had $2.00 left in my business account to provide it! :) I'm so pleased you took the time to remind me that "nothing is impossible" for you.

Thank you also for your Word that you continually use to teach me truths and comfort me while I wait expectantly for you in my desert season.

I'm still amazed that you led me to the Messianic Jewish and Gentile community where I continue to watch you reveal even greater truths and new perspectives. Today's Psalm 15 message from you made me smile - not only because I received it through a book I never would've heard about except for a referral from my Torah Club teacher - but because once again you reminded me that building my faith and character traits is far more important right now than providing me with my material wants.

I hope someday you'll allow me the honor of using my 2012 desert season story to teach others how to deepen and widen their faith in order to be more at peace in their everyday lives through being grounded in you, regardless of their circumstances.

11/28/Wed

What G_d Said:

"The Lord is my strength and my shield; *my heart trusts in him*, and I am helped. My heart leaps for joy and I will give thanks to him in song. *The Lord is the strength of his people*, a fortress of salvation for his anointed one. Save your people and bless your inheritance; be their shepherd and carry them forever." (Psalm 28:7-9)

"Master of the Universe, Who reigned before any form was created. At the time when His will brought all into being – then as 'King' was His Name proclaimed. After all has ceased to be, He, the Awesome One, will reign alone. It is He Who was, He Who is, and He Who shall remain, in splendor. He is One – there is no second to compare to Him, to declare as His equal. Without beginning, without conclusion – His is the power and dominion. *He is my God, my living Redeemer, Rock of my pain in time of distress*. He is my banner, a refuge for me, the portion of my cup on the day I call. Into His hand I shall entrust my spirit when I go to sleep – and I shall awaken! With my spirit shall my body remain. *Hashem is with me*, I shall not fear." (Adon Olam, a Jewish Morning Prayer, quoted from *Twerski on Prayer*, p. 87)

Kavannah: Hebrew word that means concentration, attention, intention, devotion, or direction. It is a state of mind that we should be striving to achieve before praying (paraphrased from *Twerski on Prayer*, p. 17-18).

What I Learned or Was Reminded About:

- You, Lord, are Master of the Universe, so what sense does it make to succumb to whatever challenges life may throw at me?

What I Prayed:

Lord – Thank you for being my strength. Without you I would never have journeyed through my desert season with a positive attitude and a deep sense of peace.

I love the Hebrew word, Kavannah, that you gave to me today. When I first read it, I was reminded of my last name (at least the way I pronounced it), and then when I saw the definition, I laughed in joy. I have no idea how to pronounce it correctly, but regardless of that I know you meant for me to be drawn to it because my whole year has been about moving closer to a Kavannah state of mind through being "still" in you!

I continue to share with my personal and professional network that despite the pain, loss, and grief I experienced all year long – I would NOT trade my desert season for anything. My growth in you through this experience is priceless and worth every second of pain I felt!

Thank you for my desert...but as you know, I am SOOOOO ready to be released from it into whatever life you have planned for me next. I hope you don't wait 40 years to deliver me (like Moses and the Israelites) – but I trust that whatever timeframe you set is the right timeframe in the long run.

11/30/Fri

<u>What G_d Said:</u>

"*But godliness with contentment is great gain. For we brought nothing into the world, and can take nothing out of it.* But if we have food and clothing, we will be content with that. People who want to get rich fall into temptation and a trap and into many foolish harmful desires that plunge men into ruin and destruction. For the love of money is a root of all kinds of evil. Some people, eager for money, have wandered from the faith and pierced themselves with many griefs. But you, man of God, flee from all this and *pursue righteousness, godliness, faith, love, endurance and gentleness.*" (1Timothy 6:6-11)

"Shout for joy to the Lord, all the earth. Worship the Lord with gladness; come before him with joyful songs. Know that the Lord is God. *It is he who made us and we are his*, we are his people, the sheep of his pasture. Enter his gates with thanksgiving and his courts with praise; give thanks to him and praise his name. *For the Lord is good and his love endures forever; his faithfulness continues through all the generations.*" (Psalm 100:1-5)

<u>What I Learned or Was Reminded About:</u>

- If I came into the world with nothing, everything I have from that point was given to me by G_d. Therefore He has the right to give me or take my "stuff" whenever He wants.

<u>What I Prayed:</u>

Lord – It's been interesting learning how to be content in circumstances I'm not happy about. However, I know it's far better to be content than to spend time fighting what is out of my control. Thank you for always meeting my needs in EVERY circumstance.

12/1/Sat & 12/2/Sun

What G_d Said:

"There remains, then, *a Sabbath rest* for the people of God; for anyone who enters God's rest also rests from his own work, just as God did from his." (Hebrews 4:9-10)

"*For the Word of God is living and active.* Shaper than any double-edged sword, it penetrates even to dividing soul and spirit, joints and marrow; it *judges the thoughts and attitudes of the heart.*" (Hebrews 4:12)

"But I am like an olive tree *flourishing in the house of God*; *I trust in God's unfailing love forever and ever.* I will praise you forever for what you have done; in your name I will hope, *for your name is good. I will praise you in the presence of your saints.*" (Psalm 52:8-9)

What I Learned or Was Reminded About:

- Honoring the Sabbath is an important part of honoring G_d.
- Spending time in G_d's Word should never feel like a chore.

What I Prayed:

Lord – Thank you for a weekly Sabbath rest…and in my case, a season of rest to focus on you, relax in your presence and study your Word which is "living and active." I continue to trust in your "unfailing love" as my desert season continues.

12/4/Tue

What G_d Said:

"And do not set your heart on what you will eat or drink; *do not worry about it*. For the pagan world runs after all such things, and *your Father knows that you need them*. But *seek the kingdom* and these things will be given to you as well." (Luke 12:29-31)

What I Learned or Was Reminded About:

- If I focus on seeking "the kingdom," everything else will fall into place in His time.

What I Prayed:

Lord – Thank you for always taking care of me, and that I do not have to worry about my basic needs because you will provide for them. I'm looking forward to seeing how things turn out in my life as a whole since my personal checkbook is dwindling fast.

As December 31st approaches, I continue to hope you'll provide me with an income high enough to get a house with a backyard so I can get my girls back. But, if not – please help me quickly push past any feelings of disappointment so I will continue to have faith that your plans are better than mine.

12/5/Wed

<u>What G_d Said:</u>

"Again, I tell you that *if two of you on earth agree about anything you ask for, it will be done for you by my Father* in heaven. For where two or three come together in my name, there am I with them." (Matthew 18:19-20)

"I know, O Lord, that *a man's life is not his own*; it is not for man to direct his steps." (Jeremiah 10:23)

<u>What I Learned or Was Reminded About:</u>

- The people who have come along side me (and I alongside them) are one of the reasons I've stayed sane and at peace during the uncertainty of my desert season.

<u>What I Prayed:</u>

Lord – Once again, I sense you reminding me that as a Believer in Jesus I must default to placing all my concerns in your care as a symbol of trust that YOU are completely in control - even though I can't always see what is happening behind the scenes of my life.

And if you ARE in control, I must allow you to "direct my steps" anywhere you choose – regardless of whether the result is victory or deliverance…or even torture, mockery, or death (Hebrews 11:33-38).

Where are you leading me? THAT is what I am waiting to find out.

When will you tell me? Soon…I hope! ☺

HOW I KEPT MY SMILE & LAUGHTER INTACT

From reading through my journal, you know it's been a rollercoaster year of emotions. When I started my journey into the desert back in February, I knew the supernatural peace G_d had granted me would carry me through – but I also knew my attitude and other people would be key factors in keeping me sane.

Ironically, back in January 2012, I had just published a new book I wrote in November 2011 called *Standing Naked in the Storm – How to produce consistent results and remain effective regardless of your circumstances*[29] (www.StandingNakedInTheStorm.com). It always amused me as I was giving my "Standing Naked in the Storm" presentations throughout 2012 to a variety of groups that I was actually living the book in my real life. I often mentioned that irony during my presentations to the shock of the audience. Reflecting back to 2011, I think G_d was preparing me for my 2012 desert season even then through the writing of that book.

The 10 "naked" qualities I discuss in the book, along with an ability to deal comfortably with three typical storm challenges, contributed to my being able to laugh and smile in the midst of my pain. Long ago I had also developed the habit of being C.E.O. of my entire life (a concept I wrote about in my previous book, *Stuck to C.E.O. – How to Take Back Control of Your Personal and Professional Life by Developing a C.E.O. Mindset*[30] / www.StucktoCEO.com) which also gave me an edge to keep moving forward despite all the moments during 2012 I wanted to crawl into a corner and hide.

When I moved about 20 minutes closer to Atlanta, I essentially moved to the other side of the earth because of traffic patterns in the area. Due to the added challenges of traffic, my support network back in Snellville was not as accessible – and I knew I needed people near me to avoid feeling so alone in my new life.

Before I moved I prayed for G_d to send me many strong Christian women who could bring joy and laughter into my world, and support me as I walked into my uncertain future. That prayer was answered quickly, and I have many stories about the women He dropped into my life in unexpected ways – some of which are still good friends today. Building a community of support is absolutely necessary to keep your smile and laughter intact during times of uncertainty.

Another key factor in keeping my smile and laughter alive was a willingness to see the absolute comedy in my situation – As an Executive and Leadership Coach, I train people all the time to maneuver through uncertainty in order to achieve their goals. What kind of Coach would I be if I couldn't do it for my own life! That, in itself, was definitely a good reminder to keep laughing and smiling as I moved forward.

From February until about August 2012, I kept a bullet point list of things I was either learning or sarcastically amused about as I journeyed through my desert. Some of those bullets are as follows:

Feb 2012
- Surreal acceptance of my peace about the loss of my marriage
- Too many memories and objects bringing about painful emotional responses
- Uncertainty in everything
- Living in separate bedrooms
- Settlement negotiations, lawyers and the law as interpreted - "fair" has many meanings!

Mar 2012
- My support network providing everything I needed as I prepared to move
- Apartment shopping - so little space for so much money!
- Serving clients while trying to take care of myself
- Standing Naked in MY storm

- Career choices – uncertainty in options
- First time going to a friend's party as a divorced woman

Apr 2012
- Seeing a dog park and crying
- Going to a new church for the first time after my divorce and crying
- Experiencing the worst birthday of my entire life (a week after the divorce was final)
- Working out the visitation rights for the dogs and complications that unexpectedly arose along the way
- Not seeing the dogs every day
- Living alone for the first time in nine years
- Getting a ticket for an "unlawful U-Turn" the first week I moved to my apartment…$150.00 wasted!
- Getting to know my nice neighbors and being thankful the apartment complex was quiet

May 2012
- Throwing my first party at my apartment with many of my old and new friends
- Walking around my apartment in a daze wondering what my future holds
- Experiencing a few "country song" moments that made me cry and laugh at the same time!
- Feeling completely out of control

June 2012
- A new friend's philosophy about the "why?" rabbit hole and how it ties you to the circumstance instead of setting you free
- Too much time on my hands, but having nowhere to go and nothing to do
- Craving a visit home (metro-NYC), but not having the money to go

- Unexpected business income allowing me to pay business bills I thought I wouldn't be able to pay
- Treating myself to getting my nails done; something I haven't done in a very long time
- Being part of the Oasis Divorce Recovery Group and thankful I could lean on them as needed.

July 2012
- Wondering when God will restore all that's been lost in my life
- Noticing that because I'm divorced I don't fit in anywhere right now – most of the groups or friends I have currently have kids, which makes it very hard for them to be available to hang out spontaneously.

Aug 2012
- How weird it felt being called "Mrs." Cavanaugh, and not wanting to spend the energy to correct anyone
- Listening to people talk about their anniversaries…and suddenly feeling sad that I won't be celebrating mine this year
- Leaving the house and seeing the dogs poke their noses under the gate, and suddenly crying because I have to leave…then feeling annoyed at how unfair it is that Danny has the dogs instead of me
- A solid job lead appears, and then disappears three weeks later
- First time having to see Danny with another woman

In every situation above, I could have focused on my pain, burrowed into my sadness, and gotten lost in my emotions. I chose NOT to walk that path. Instead I overcame my pain, walked through my sadness, and managed my emotions as well as I could one day at a time. And that is why I was able to laugh and keep my smile intact!

THE END OF MY STORY ?

At this moment in time I am still walking in uncertainty, my checkbook is dwindling fast, and I have no job leads (I am hoping the reason I have no leads is because G_d might resurrect my business in some way).

How does my story end? Only G_d knows, but here's the really amazing thing – *it doesn't matter what happens*. If I believe G_d is Lord of my life (and I do!), I can deal with whatever shows up.

I still pray every day for G_d to restore all that I lost by providing the income to purchase a house with a yard so I can get my dogs back – that hasn't changed. What has changed is that I moved from understanding submission to my Lord as a concept to now KNOWING it as a reality. That lesson alone is priceless!

I'm sure I still have more lessons to learn in my desert, but I'm certain I have gained a stronger foundation in my faith just in the last two months - and I wouldn't trade this time in the desert for all the money in the world!

I am blessed beyond measure with spiritual treasures that no one can take from me. Earthly treasures will come and go – don't ever forget that!

As I close out this book, I want to wish you all the best in <u>your</u> future as you maneuver through your own life challenges or desert seasons. I also want to leave you with a verse to encourage you every day of your life:

"And we rejoice in the hope of the glory of God. Not only so, but also rejoice in our sufferings, because we know that suffering produces perseverance; perseverance, character; and character, hope!" (Romans 5:2b-4)

Sincerely,
Kris Cavanaugh

Beloved Daughter of He who knew me before He formed me in my mother's womb! (Jeremiah 1:5A)

FINAL THOUGHTS

Thank you for taking the time to journey with me through my desert season by reading this book. I hope you felt it was a valuable use of your time.

If you know of other people who could benefit from reading *Be Still? Really, Lord??,* here are some ways you can share the information with others:

- ◊ Purchase extra copies of the book to pass out to your personal and professional network as G_d leads (buy online at www.BeStill-ReallyGod.com). Discounts are available for bulk purchases of 25 or more books (call 404-551-3601 for discount pricing).
- ◊ Share the book website through your Facebook, LinkedIn, and Twitter accounts (www.BeStill-ReallyGod.com).
- ◊ Share your "Be Still" story (click on tab titled "Share your Be Still Story" on www.BeStill-ReallyGod.com).
- ◊ Arrange to have me speak to your organization.
- ◊ Write a testimony on Amazon.com.

If I can be of service to you in any way, feel free to contact me at Info@BeginToShift.com.

COACHING & TRAINNG

> *I currently have no idea whether my business is closed for good, or whether G_d wanted to shut it down during my desert season to force me to be dependent on Him. Should the latter be the case (that continues to be my hope!), below is information about my coaching and training business to pass onto anyone you think may benefit from it. Thanks!* ☺

Successful relationships are built on shared goals or objectives. *I am a good coach for anyone who desires produce more consistent results and increase their effectiveness in their life and work.* They understand the importance of investing in their future and know a strong, structured support system with measurable goals and attainable outcomes could make it happen.

My objective as your coach is to help you SHIFT from where you are now (personally and professionally) to where you want to be as quickly as possible. To learn more, read "Why Choose a Coaching Program" below.

If you are interested in chatting further about having me deliver a keynote program to your group, call me at 404-551-3601 so we can talk in more detail.

WHY CHOOSE A COACHING PROGRAM?

The value of working with a coach is that I actively listen to you, ask powerful questions, add objective observations, and support you in developing a strategy that transforms your personal or professional world into whatever you want it to be through:

1. Inspiring new vision by thinking outside the box.
2. Improving thinking and decision making skills.
3. Helping discover new life options and perspectives.
4. Assisting with defining and moving through obstacles.

5. Learning ways to handle stress.
6. Regaining confidence by demolishing the negative mindset holding you back.
7. Clarifying what really matters in your life.
8. Providing encouragement, motivation, and accountability.

As an experienced strategist for over 20 years, and member of the International Coach Federation, I have been coaching individuals who aspire to better themselves personally and professionally.

As my mission statement says, I am *"Dedicated to empowering others to live their lives believing they can overcome any obstacle to achieve their personal and professional goals and dreams."*

Coaching, which should not be confused with mentoring or training, focuses on your present and future goals and behaviors rather than emotions and emotional patterns. I will teach you essential skills to confront challenges head-on, enabling you to more easily weather life's storms and achieve the personal goals and dreams you may never have thought possible.

Three Common Concerns

If you have connected to the information in this book and truly desire to make significant changes in your life, you may have one of the following concerns when considering a coaching program:

1. I don't understand the value of a coaching program.
2. I don't' have time to fit in a coaching program
3. I don't have the money to invest in a coaching program.

Each of these questions is answered in a document you can download here:

www.begintoshift.com/3-common-concerns.pdf

WHAT IS THE NEXT STEP?

If you are ready to invest in yourself in order to manage your life more effectively, **schedule an "Exploration Meeting" with me** to determine if I am the right coach to make that happen.

You can schedule that meeting by calling me at 404-551-3601 or by going to the following website: **http://www.begintoshift.com/pages/maketheshift**.

ABOUT KRIS CAVANAUGH & SHIFT

As a Speaker, Trainer, Facilitator, and ICF certified Coach, Kris Cavanaugh's background includes over 20 years of experience training and mentoring individuals. She believes the key to a successful life begins with a person's ability to become C.E.O of their entire life and stand "naked" in their storms. Kris is an expert strategist with an amazing ability to pull her clients through difficult challenges to obtain the results they truly desire.

Her company, Shift, specializes in helping individuals and companies *produce more consistent results* and *increase their effectiveness* so their businesses, organizations, departments, and personal lives thrive. Her clients experience a higher quality of life by the end of her coaching programs, allowing them to gain a deeper sense of well-being and satisfaction both personally and professionally.

If you have a desire to live your life "on purpose" so you wake up every day excited about the possibilities and maintain an unwavering belief that you will overcome any obstacles to achieve your personal and professional goals more easily and consistently, Kris would be a wonderful resource for you to connect with to make that happen. To learn more about Kris Cavanaugh and Shift, please go to www.BeginToShift.com.

Kris looks forward to developing relationships with all her clients, and truly loves watching their lives transform dramatically during the coaching process. There is nothing better to Kris than knowing every day she has a chance to make a difference in the world around her – one life at a time!

Testimonies about Kris include:

"For a long time I put off the notion of hiring an Executive Coach, even though there are many books and professionals that swear by it. When I decided to hire Kris, it was an easy decision. She is one of the most positive people I know and from initial strategy discussions to coaching calls; she had questions and solutions that were completely out-of-the-box. I admire how she can take a problem and break it down to a process. Process is something I am excellent at in business, but she has helped me see how I can apply it to my personal life as well."
- Todd Nielsen, CEO, Decision Systems Plus, Inc.

"One of our IT Managers referred Kris to us as a speaker for our Women of AT&T luncheon. Her interactive presentation proved to be very insightful and valuable to everyone in the room. Several employees thanked me afterwards for inviting Kris to speak and suggested we have her come back for another event. I would highly recommend Kris to any company seeking to motivate their employees to be their best because she has a natural way of helping them "connect the dots" and providing strategic tools to make it happen."
- Theresa Spralling, Senior Associate Director of Training, AT&T

To hear what others have said, go to www.BeginToShift.com.

LEGAL DISCLAIMER

The author and publisher of this book and the accompanying materials have used their best efforts in preparing this book. The information contained in this book is *strictly* for educational purposes. Therefore, if you wish to apply ideas contained in this book, you are taking full responsibility for your actions.

Your level of success in attaining the results claimed in our materials depends on the time you devote to the program, ideas and techniques mentioned, your finances, knowledge and various skills. Since these factors differ according to individuals, we cannot guarantee your success. Nor are we responsible for any of your actions. Many factors *will* be important in determining your actual results and no guarantees are made that you will achieve results similar to ours or anybody else's, in fact no guarantees are made that you will achieve any results from our ideas and techniques in our material.

The author and publisher disclaim any warranties (express or implied), merchantability, or fitness for any particular purpose. The author and publisher shall in no event be held liable to any party for any direct, indirect, punitive, special, incidental or other consequential damages arising directly or indirectly from any use of this material, which is provided "as is", and without warranties.

The author and publisher do not warrant the performance, effectiveness or applicability of any sites listed or linked to in this report. *All* links are for information purposes only and are not warranted for content, accuracy or any other implied or explicit purpose.

This book is © (copyrighted) by Shift Inc. No part of this may be copied, or changed in any format, sold, or used in any way without permission.

RESOURCES CITED

[1] All Bible Verses, unless noted otherwise, are taken from the New International Version (NIV).

[2] *Rabbinical Halakhah – Writing the Hebrew Names of God.* Retrieved from: http://www.hebrew4christians.com/Names_of_G-d/About_Writing/about_writing.html.

[3] All Dictionary references are from http://www.Merriam-Webster.com.

[4] To find a Messianic Congregation in your area, go to: http://www.manna.com/index.html.

[5] Beth Adonai (means "House of G_d"), a Messianic Congregation where Jews and Gentiles worship together: http://www.bethadonai.com.

[6] Torah Portions cycle can be downloaded here (Note: Hebrew Year 5773 = calendar year 2012-2013): http://ffoz.org/downloads/torah_study_resources or at http://torahportions.org. Messianic Torah Portions include readings from the first five books of the Bible, the Haftarah (prophets) and the Gospel. In traditional Jewish culture (non-Messianic) the Torah cycle does not include the Gospel portions.

[7] *HaYesod – The Foundation* can be experienced as a group or individually. I chose to go through the program through Beth Adonai. To learn more about this program, visit the website: http://hayesod.org.

[8] First Fruits of Zion (2012). *HaYesod, The Foundation.* Marshfield, MO: First Fruits of Zion.

[9] Greenfield, R. (2008). *The Servant as Leader.* Westfield, IN: The Greenleaf Center for Servant Leadership.

[10] Blackaby, H., Blackaby R., King, C (2008). *Experiencing God – Knowing and Doing the Will of God* (Revised & Expanded Version). Nashville, TN: B&H Publishing Group. (For you Amazon lovers like myself, type in product #0805447539)

[11] *Wisdom Hunters* daily devotional: http://www.wisdomhunters.com.

[12] *The Upper Room* daily devotional: http://devotional.upperroom.org.

[13] *Torah Club* samples can be downloaded at the First Fruits of Zion website here: http://torahclub.org

[14] Cowman, L.B. (1997). *Streams in the Desert – 365 Daily Devotional Readings.* Grand Rapids, MI: Zondervan. This book was first published in 1925 and re-edited several times since then.

[15] Sharon Jaynes Blog Post: http://sharonjaynes.com

[16] McLean, C (2012). *Learning to Live Above* – Learning to Live an Abundant Life in an Everyday World. Dacula, GA: Art Book Bindery.

[17] Blackaby, H., Blackaby R., King, C (2007). *Experiencing God – Knowing and Doing the Will of God* (Revised & Expanded Version of the companion workbook). Nashville, TN: LifeWay Press

[18] Author Unknown. *God's Promises to His Children.* Retrieved from: http://www.smilegodlovesyou.org/promises.html

[19] Prince, D (1975). *Appointment in Jerusalem – by Lydia Prince as told to her husband, Derek Prince.* Charlotte, NC: Derek Prince Ministries – International

[20] Copeland, G (1997 Commemorative Edition). *Prayers That Avail Much.* Roswell, GA: Word Ministries Inc.

[21] *Saving Faith* sermon series (May 2012). Pastor Rodney Anderson and Pastor Brent Shoemaker from Buckhead Church / North Point Church community: Retrieved from: http://npmsingles.org/series/summer-singles-series-saving-faith/?campus=buckhead

[22] Oasis Divorce Recovery Group through Andy Stanley's church community: http://www.buckheadchurch.org/oasis

[23] *Matthew Henry's Commentary* on Philippians 4:11-13: http://www.biblegateway.com/resources/matthew-henry/Phil.4.10-Phil.4.19

[24] *Owned* sermon series (September – October 2012). Pastor Joel Thomas and Pastor Clay Scroggins from Buckhead Church / North Point Church community. Retrieved from: http://www.northpoint.org/messages/owned

[25] YouTube video of *While I'm Waiting* (a song by John Waller) can be found at: http://www.youtube.com/watch?v=Bb7TSGptd3Y&feature=youtube_gdata_player

[26] *Be Rich* sermon series (November 2012). Pastor Andy Stanley at North Point Church: Retrieved from: http://www.northpoint.org/messages/how-to-be-rich-2012

[27] Sheets, D. (1996). *Intercessory Prayer – How God Can Use Your Prayers to Move Heaven and Earth*. Ventura, CA: Regal Books.

[28] Twerski, A. (2004). *Twerski on Prayer – Creating the Bond Between Man and His Maker*. New York, NY: Shaar Press.

[29] Cavanaugh, K. (2012). *Standing Naked in the Storm – How to produce consistent results and remain effective regardless of your circumstances.*. Atlanta, GA: Shift Inc.

[30] Cavanaugh, K. (2010). *Stuck to C.E.O. – How to Take Back Control of Your Personal and Professional Life by Developing a C.E.O. Mindset*. Atlanta, GA: Shift Inc.